Getting the Picture Right

In Your Marriage

SCOTT T. BROWN

Church &
Family Life

Getting the Picture Right in Your Marriage
by Scott T. Brown
First Printing: January 2024

Church & Family Life
220 South White St., Wake Forest, NC 27587
www.churchandfamilylife.com

ISBN: 978-1-62418-068-2
Cover Design and Typography by Justin Turley
Printed in the United States of America

I dedicate these words to Deborah

who has been such a comfortable and pleasant wife

making me always want to come home

Contents

Introduction

Every marriage paints pictures.

The question is: What kind of picture are you painting as husband and wife? What are the people doing in the portrait? What is the backdrop? What sort of images and aromas does your painting display?

Thankfully, we are not left to ourselves to learn how to paint. God through His Word and by His Spirit comes alongside to help us learn to paint beautifully. He teaches us to paint pictures that reflect the beauty of His light and truth, and the emanations of His wonderful attributes.

From Genesis to Revelation, God gives us beautiful pictures of what marriage was intended to be. He gives us striking portraits that are rich with symbolism and meaning.

In this book you will find eleven such pictures of marriage. These vivid images are more than mere metaphor—they contain sacred truths designed to shape and guide how husbands and wives are to relate to one another in marriage. They show us how to paint beautifully.

Whether you are married or desiring to enter wedlock one day, the goal of this book is to bring these pictures to life—to place them at the front of your eyes and thoughts and in the center of your heart.

To the extent you get these pictures right and frame your marriage after their fashion, your wedded life will be blessed and flourish.

Marriage Is a Picture of Joy

Joy is an essential picture you'll encounter as you make your way through this book, and you will read various citations from Jonathan Edwards' work, *The End for Which God Created the World*, that illustrate this portrait.[1]

Why?

Over the years, I've come to believe that God's ultimate objective is to rescue sinners in order to bring them into His everlasting kingdom of joy, where His joy is the center of all things. It flows from His Being "on earth as it is in heaven" (Matt. 6:10).

This has everything to do with a marriage.

> . . . *when God's happiness overflows from the core of his being into the lives of other creatures, they have the privilege of participating in the happiness God has in himself. After all, God and his glory provide the objective ground of true happiness.*[2]

This theme runs throughout this book and is explained in detail in the second chapter, "Rejoicing in Marriage: The First Year and Beyond."

Edwards states it like this:

> *Scripture teaches that God's ultimate end for creating the world was to pour out his goodness upon his people, the eternal subjects of his goodness, by giving them the whole of creation, every part of it.*[3]

Marriage is an institution which is designed to be filled by His ever-flowing fountain of joy:

---

1 Jonathan Edwards, *The End for Which the God Created the World: Updated in Modern English,* ed. Jason Dollar (Jason Dollar, 2018), Kindle. Hereafter cited as "Edwards."

2 Edwards, p. 75.

3 Edwards, p. 205.

... by flowing forth his light and glory and expressing himself to them and in them, he makes them partake of him. He then rejoices in himself as expressed in them, delighting in his perfect attributes and glory communicated to and through them.[4]

Hug Your Honey

Embracing is another picture vital to marriage. King Solomon frames it this way: There is "a time to embrace, and a time to refrain from embracing" (Eccl. 3:5).

Here's the takeaway: If you are married, you are *not* in the time of your life to refrain from embracing. Those days are gone; those were the single years. You are in a new season with a new priority—you are to freely and lovingly embrace your spouse. I am here to explain what it looks like to embrace.

I learned this well from my father. My dad would often say to me, "Son, hug your honey."

He did not mean just to go give your wife a hug.

It included hugging her, but he meant far more than just a hug. He meant, "Pay attention; spend time with; don't be so busy."

He meant, "Smell the roses!"

In that statement my dad was rolling up the beauty of marriage. He was mobilizing me to nourish, cherish, wash, sanctify, and sacrifice. All the words of Ephesians 5:22-33 were loaded in that statement.

I later learned that my dad delivered this admonition to dozens of men—including most of the married men in our church. One man told me that my dad said this to him at least twenty times over the years.

What my dad said to me and to other husbands is also applicable to wives. "Hug your honey" goes both ways. Even as the bride is to be taken by the bridegroom—"His left hand

---

4 Edwards, p. 113.

is under my head, And his right hand embraces me" (Song of Sol. 2:6)—she is to return this warm gesture, "I am my beloved's, and my beloved is mine" (Song of Sol. 6:3).

My dad loved my mother. And my mother loved her husband. They had a happy marriage. And, my dad was a happy man. One day, we were riding in a car to a father son retreat in the mountains of Colorado, and our friend Bill Roach asked my dad about his upcoming 60th wedding anniversary, "Bill, are you gonna have a shindig?" Dad replied, "Bill, everyday's a shindig." That was his version of "hug your honey."

While husbands and wives have distinctive roles, there is a thread that runs through these roles which ties both husband and wife together. What ties them together are cords of love, displayed in pictures.

This arresting imagery was modeled by our Lord Himself. As He has drawn us to Himself with "bands of love" (Hos. 11:4), so we as married couples are to draw each other close.

I am extremely grateful to learn this picture of embracing from my father. I pray you will prayerfully seek to emulate it in your married life, along with the other gripping pictures of marriage found in this book.

Let us "not [be] disobedient to the heavenly vision" (Acts 26:19), but rather showcase this beauty in joyful marriages before a watching world.

Scott Brown
Wake Forest, NC
December 2023

CHAPTER I

Marriage Is Sacred Space

'For this reason a man shall leave his father and mother and be joined to his wife, and the two shall become one flesh.' This is a great mystery, but I speak concerning Christ and the church. (Eph. 5:31-32)

Marriage changes our state of being. You pass from one realm (singleness) to another (marriage). As we pass from singleness into marriage, we leave father and mother and are joined in marriage—"the LORD's holy institution which He loves" (Mal. 2:11).

Going into a marriage is like going to the White House. You are on someone else's property. You don't get to do what you want. Similarly, when you dine with the Queen of England, you're not free to eat any way you please. You eat the way you are supposed to eat when you sup with royalty.

Marriage is like that. You are a visitor in God's "holy institution" (Mal. 2:11). You come as an outsider to something that does not belong to you. You did not create it. It was gift. You are simply a steward at somebody else's estate. You are like a servant in the realm of a King. You are a manager of a property not your own. And, it is not yours forever—only for your time on earth—"For in the resurrection they neither marry nor are given in marriage, but are like angels of God in heaven" (Matt. 22:30).

Marriage Is Sacred Space

When you enter into marriage, you are on God's turf. It does not exist for your own pleasure.

Marriage is sacred space. It is sacred because it was designed by God. His plan is to include you in demonstrating a mystery—the mystery of Christ's everlasting love for His church (Eph. 5:31-32).

This means that you are a visitor in Christ's institution. Marriage belongs to Him. He gave it rules and boundaries; it's His space. So you're not free to tinker with matrimony and make up our own way. You are to honor it as a set apart estate.

At a Neighbor's Home: On Good Behavior

The concept of sacred space is familiar to all of us. We acknowledge it regularly. When we visit a neighbor, a business, or a church, we don't act any old way. Because the place is not ours, we thoughtfully behave.

Here is an illustration. When your kids cross the threshold of a neighbor's house, they go into another jurisdiction. They enter sacred space. If you are a good parent, you know that your children must be taught that they are not allowed to do their own thing in someone else's home.

- They must enter respectfully
- They must proceed quietly
- They must not run
- They must not crawl on the furniture
- They must not touch things on tables
- They must not open drawers
- They must not rifle through the toys
- They must not sit on the dinner table

- They must not snoop around
- They must talk respectfully
- They must engage their hosts with eye contact
- They must not tease the dog
- They must exit graciously

If your kids don't play by the rules of propriety, they may make a mess. They may offend the homeowner. The same goes for your marriage. There is a way you are to conduct yourself in this sacred space. You are not your own. There are rules to follow, and God made them. When you break these rules and act selfishly, you disrupt the institutional purpose.

Bad Manners from a Bad Heart

Here is the problem: everyone who enters into God's institution of marriage brings a mixture of bad baggage with them, including:

- Bad manners
- Selfish motives
- Flawed patterns
- Dull consciences
- Worldly ideas
- Wrong ideas about manhood and womanhood
- Secular inclinations about sex
- Whatever else

Why? We live in a fallen world, and we've gotten used to following our hearts over the Word of God.

This is a dangerous bowl of soup, for, "The heart is deceitful above all things, And desperately wicked; Who can know it?" (Jer. 17:9).

Trusting our hearts is sheer folly. Moses declared that the person who boasts that he's following his own heart is like a "drunkard" (Deut. 29:19). Solomon was equally as blunt: "He who trusts in his own heart is a fool" (Prov. 28:26).

Whenever we fail to govern our hearts and enthrone self, what comes forth will be harmful, "Out of the heart come evil thoughts, For out of the heart proceed evil thoughts, murders, adulteries, fornications, thefts, false witness, blasphemies" (Matt. 15:19).

This heart-struggle goes to the core of our sinful state.

As fallen creatures, we have a sin nature that—if left uncleansed—will taint everything we think, feel, and do. Apart from Christ, we will walk in the flesh, not the Spirit. Without His enabling grace, our consciences (the voices in our heads that tell us what is right) will remain disfigured, and our desires will be out of order.

Whenever our hearts remain in sin's grip, harmful impulses will drive our behaviors and frame our expectations in relation to happiness, satisfaction, pleasure, sex, and relationships.

Left to our natural selves, we will bring all these wrong views of love and marriage into married life. This includes bad patterns we've adopted and bad role models we've admired.

Even if God has saved us, we will still have bad baggage to deal with. Some of this baggage will come from who we were in our unredeemed state, yet some will come from carnal patterns we've coddled and cultivated, even while being a true Christian.

Hope in the New Birth

But all is not lost—by God's grace, we can begin to treat marriage as sacred space. We can change our bad manners. The good news is that the power of sin is broken by the new birth (Rom. 6:5-10). We can "walk in newness of life" (Rom. 6:4). Though once dead, we can have "life [in] our mortal bodies" (Rom. 8:11). As a result, the overflow of our hearts can be cleansed.

This begins by turning to Christ in faith (Eph. 2:8-9; Rom. 10:9) and repenting of our sins, "Repent you therefore, and be converted, that your sins may be blotted out . . ." (Acts 3:19). "If we confess our sins, He is faithful and just to forgive us our sins and to cleanse us from all unrighteousness" (1 John 1:9).

Pursue Sanctification

Once we've become new creatures through regeneration (2 Cor. 5:17; John 3:5-8), we must pursue sanctification through a delight in the Scriptures. Filling our heart with God's Word will reshape our consciences, emotions, and desires, "Your word I have hidden in my heart, That I might not sin against You!" (Ps. 119:11).

When this occurs, our hearts will flow with good rather than bad manners:

> *A good man out of the good treasure of his heart brings forth good; and an evil man out of the evil treasure of his heart brings forth evil. For out of the abundance of the heart his mouth speaks. (Luke 6:45)*

Sanctification will not happen overnight. It took us awhile to dig the hole—shovel by shovel. It will take some time to fill it up—one shovel at a time. It is a progressive process. Sometimes we take two steps forward and one step back, but we must strive, each day, to be more set apart in our behavior.

This means, "He must increase, but [we] must decrease" (John 3:30). This is how the Lord designed your marriage— more of Christ and His Spirit and less of you. This is the essence of the true believer.

Renounce Your Ways, Crucify the Flesh

A Christian is a person who has renounced his own ways. He wants to follow Jesus. Not his personal version of love. Not his emotions. Not his habits. Not his background. Not his baggage.

A true Christian will long to crucify those things that do not please his Lord:

> *And those who are Christ's have crucified the flesh with its passions and desires. If we live in the Spirit, let us also walk in the Spirit. Let us not become conceited, provoking one another, envying one another. (Gal. 5:24-26)*

To have a Christian marriage, you must understand that you are not your own. Marriage is not your property—it is God's—and you are dwelling in His sacred space. You must therefore cast aside your old life, your sinful passions and desires (Eph. 4:22), and "walk in the Spirit" (Gal. 5:16).

This is how you are to behave.

So don't stay as you are. Obey God's house rules instead. Marriage belongs to Him, and you have the duty to make your marriage what He meant it to be.

As you are getting the picture right, learn to paint a beautiful picture of a sacred, protected space where you are a steward and servant in God's holy institution.

Questions

1. Can you identify behaviors, manners, presuppositions, and expectations you brought into marriage that are contrary to God's design?

2. Can you explain the wrong view of love you acquired along the way in your life?

CHAPTER 2

———◆———

Rejoicing in Marriage:
The First Year and Beyond

When a man has taken a new wife, he shall not go out to war or be charged with any business; he shall be free at home one year, and bring happiness to his wife whom he has taken. (Deut. 24:5)

In the biblical picture of marriage, you find a joyful couple. The first thing that happened at the first marriage was an outburst of joy, as Adam poetically declared:

This is now bone of my bones
And flesh of my flesh;
She shall be called Woman,
Because she was taken out of Man. (Gen. 2:23)

A husband is called by God to brighten up his wife (Deut. 24:5). The very Creator of matrimony delivered a law that facilitates a couples' joyful bonding together during their first year of wedlock (Deut. 24:5). From this we learn that God wants to see happiness in marriages. This is the result of Christlikeness.

Jonathan Edwards states:

When the creature displays excellent qualities and happiness, it is nothing more than the expressions of God's glory shining in and through them. Thus, in seeking their glory and happiness, God makes himself his own ultimate end (that is, himself diffused and shining outwardly, which he delights in just as he delights in his innate beauty and fullness), he seeks their glory and happiness as well.[1]

---

1   Edwards, 109.

Start Well, Establish Good Patterns

Husbands must take the lead in starting well. The first weeks and months of your marriage are critical. During this time, you form patterns that will either nourish or deprive your future as a couple.

What a man does with the first year of his wife's life with him will have a profound effect on her over the long-term. If he acts harshly toward her, hurts her, and neglects her early on, she may have a very difficult time recovering. Bitterness is a hard case. She may become "harder to win than a strong city," and her heart may become like "bars of a castle," as the writer of Proverbs warns (Prov. 18:19).

How you establish your marriage and family life will have powerful consequences. We are creatures of habit, so it is important that we do not create bad patterns, for they can easily become destructive ruts.

I was born in Alaska, and it was only a decade before I was born that the Alaska Highway came to be. It was called the Alcan Highway. It was built during WWII to connect the lower 48 states with Alaska. The construction of this 1700-mile road was accelerated when Japan invaded the Aleutian Islands. It was a dangerous road. Before it was paved, there was reportedly a sign posted at the start of one rough stretch which read, "Choose your rut carefully—you'll be in it for the next 200 miles."[2]

Abrasive ruts will only cause harm. A couple should thus make forming good rather than bad habits a priority as they start their marriage.

2　As quoted in Ben Patterson, *Praying the Psalms: Drawing Near to the Heart of God* (Carol Stream, IL: Tyndale House Publishers, 2017), p. 211.

"Thou Shalt Not Steal": The Joy of Marriage Must Be Preserved

In Deuteronomy 24:5, a law was put in force so that the state could not hold back a husband from bringing joy to his wife during their first year of wedded life:

> *When a man has taken a new wife, he shall not go out to war or be charged with any business; he shall be free at home one year, and bring happiness to his wife whom he has taken. (Deut. 24:5)*

This law teaches the state not to steal from a young married couple. It does this by commanding a husband to spend the first year of his marriage making his wife happy, for it steals the happiness of a wife for a husband to be absent as they begin their married life together.

A Call to Husbands: Cheer Up Your Wife

Why is it so important for a husband to cheer up his wife in their first year of marriage?

For one, her life changes more than her husband's, as she moves from one family to the next and must learn to follow him as her new family leader. Leaving and cleaving requires ample one-on-one time that will be short-changed if a husband disappears for big chunks of time. Such a spotty start can be greatly discouraging to a newly married woman.

Many years ago, I heard Jeff Pollard say something I cannot forget, "Are you relating to your wife in a way that makes her sorry she is a woman?" Not working as a husband to cheer your wife up and devoting ample time to her personal needs will bring such frustration to her soul.

This does not mean that newlyweds should be so self-absorbed that they become hermit crabs. Acting this way will cut the couple off from other relationships and the beneficial flow of the fellowship of the saints. Wrong conclusions might be: "We don't want to share one another with anyone else. We need to pull out of everything and focus on ourselves." The command for a man to focus on his wife's happiness during their first year together is significant, yet it should not lead them to forget hospitality and neglect the numerous "one another" mandates found in Scripture.

Yet this law emphatically gives the family higher priority than the needs of the state. No concern of the state should get in the way of marital happiness. Therefore, the husband should not be inducted into military service during his first year of married life.

I do not believe that this law restricts a husband from working, but it seems to focus the man's time chiefly on his wife. John Gill, quoting Maimonides, says the law was even applied in Israel to free husbands from taxation for a year. In one known case it was honored by the Greeks. Aristotle is said to have learned this law from a Jew and then taught it to Alexander the Great. After the Battle of Granicus, Alexander sent his newly-married men home to be with their wives over the winter.[3]

At its very heart, I believe this law conveys a principle that should be carried forward to every year of marriage—not just the first. This enduring, lifelong principle is expressed well by Solomon:

> *Let your fountain be blessed, and rejoice with the wife of your youth. As a loving deer and a graceful doe, let her breasts satisfy you at all times; and always be enraptured with her love. (Prov. 5:18)*

The principle found here is that marriage was made for happiness, so make your love a joy all the years you have with one another: "Live joyfully with the wife whom you love all the days of your vain life which He has given you under the sun" (Eccl. 9:9).

---

3 Both the Maimonides and Alexander the Great examples are cited by John Gill in his commentary on Deut. 24:5: John Gill, *An Exposition of the Old Testament, Vol. II* (London: Mathews and Leigh, 1810), p. 104.

Rejoicing from Day One On

While God commands a husband to make his wife happy in the first year of matrimony, this does not mean that he stops after their one-year anniversary. He is to get the ball rolling over the first twelve months, yet he ought to keep it rolling every day of his marriage. Joy is God's design for married life.

God often speaks through repetition. When something in the Bible is repeated over and over again, we ought to pay attention. All throughout the Scripture, where some aspect of a wedding is described or implied, there is one idea that dominates: joy or rejoicing (Gen 2:22-25; Ps. 19:4-6; Ps. 45:1-17; Song of Sol. 3:11; Isa. 49:18; Isa. 61:10; Isa. 62:5; Jer. 2:32; Jer. 25:10; Jer. 33:11; Zeph. 3:17; Matt. 22:3-12; ; Luke 5:34; John 3:29; Rom 14:17; Rev. 18:23; Rev. 19:7-9; Rev. 21:2-4).

This is why I believe you can sum up the outcome of everything God intended for marriage in a three-letter-word—joy!

Christ Rejoicing Over His Bride

Entering into marriage is one of the most important things a human being ever does, because of what it represents. It is a picture of Christ and His church. It is based on a lifelong covenant designed to display the love of Jesus Christ for His bride, the church. He Himself is the bridegroom.

Christ models joy in marriage. Like every bridegroom in the Bible, He rejoices in matrimony. He is "anointed with the oil of gladness above all His companions" (Heb. 1:9, NASB). He rejoices over His bride with singing (Zeph. 3:17).

A Wedding Is a Metaphor

The theme of the Bible is to display God's rescue of a bride for Himself, so it makes sense that weddings are metaphors for joy in the love of Christ for His church.

Marriages are meant for joy. The joy of earthly marriage is a foretaste of our heavenly union with Christ. The Bible begins and ends with a wedding. It begins with the exultation of Adam in his bride, as he broke out in poetry when God brought him Eve as his wife (Gen. 2:23). The Bible ends with the Marriage Supper of the Lamb, where joy is gladly exclaimed (Rev. 19:6-9). Joy is on display from the first wedding in the Bible to the last.

Weddings in the Bible are described with the language of joy. From bride to bridegroom, to the attendants, joy is the theme. The day of a wedding is a day of gladness.

King Solomon's wedding was described as such a day:

Go forth, O daughters of Zion, and see King Solomon with the crown with which his mother crowned him on the day of his wedding, the day of the gladness of his heart. (Song of Sol. 3:11)

Both Bridegroom and Bride Voice Their Joy

In the Scriptures, the bridegroom and bride don't hide their joy. They voice it openly, praising God for His goodness and everlasting mercy:

[T]he voice of joy and the voice of gladness, the voice of the bridegroom and the voice of the bride, the voice of those who will say: "Praise the LORD of hosts, For the LORD is good, For His mercy endures forever." (Jer. 33:11)

The Joy of the Bridegroom

In Psalm 19:4-6, the sun is compared to a bridegroom coming out of his chamber. It is a picture of manly joy. The sun coming up is unstoppable in the same way a bridegroom is unstoppable. He "rejoices as a strong man to run his race" to the end.

In them He has set a tabernacle for the sun, Which is like a bridegroom coming out of his chamber, And rejoices like a strong man to run its race. Its rising is from one end of heaven, And its circuit to the other end. (Ps. 19:4-6)

The Joy of the Bride

Weddings are celebrations. The bride and groom are rejoicing. They are arrayed in beautiful clothing. They are covered with glory, and their outward appearances bear witness to the realities of joy.

In Isaiah 61:10, the bride expresses great joy for her garments of salvation, given to her by her groom:

I will greatly rejoice in the Lord, My soul shall be joyful in my God; For He has clothed me with the garments of salvation, He has covered me with the robe of righteousness, As a bridegroom decks himself with ornaments, And as a bride adorns herself with her jewels. (Isa. 61:10)

History's Final Wedding: A Supper of Rejoicing

History's final wedding is marked by joy, as the great host in attendance rejoices together at the Wedding Supper of the Lamb:

And I heard, as it were, the voice of a great multitude, as the sound of many waters and as the sound of mighty thunderings, saying, "Alleluia! For the Lord God Omnipotent reigns! Let us be glad and rejoice and give Him glory, for the marriage of the Lamb has come, and His wife has made herself ready." And to her it was granted to be arrayed in fine linen, clean and bright, for the fine linen is the righteous acts of the saints. Then he said to me, "Write: 'Blessed are those who are called to the marriage supper of the Lamb!'" And he said to me, "These are the true sayings of God." (Rev. 19:6-9)

The Spirit of Marriage Is a Spirit of Joy

The spirit of marriage is a spirit of joy. This is the testimony found in all of Scripture.

One's wedding day is to be characterized by gladness, husbands are called to cheer up their wives up during their first year of wedlock (Deut. 24:5), and joy should shine throughout all of one's marriage, "Live joyfully with the wife whom you love all the days of your vain life which He has given you under the sun" (Eccl. 9:9).

This is simply a reflection of the attributes of God emanating in a husband and wife as they live out their lives together:

> *God is infinitely full of all possible good. He possesses every perfect attribute to its greatest possible measure. He has as his very nature all excellence and beauty, and he is infinitely happy. Furthermore, all of this fullness is capable of overflowing from God's being. That is, he is able to communicate his fullness. He can emanate all of his goodness and glory outward to others. It seems agreeable, desirable, and valuable that it should flow. It is right, proper, and fitting for the infinite fountain of good to pour out into abundant streams!*[4]

True joy is a fruit of the Holy Spirit (Gal. 6:22), so to keep and maintain joy in our married life, we must "be filled with the Spirit" (Eph. 5:18).

Finally:

> *God's happiness consists in the enjoyment of himself. The happiness of the creatures also consists in the enjoyment of God. In fact, all true happiness is derived from rejoicing in the being, attributes, and actions of God. As with knowledge and holiness, when God's happiness overflows from the core of his being into the lives of other creatures, they have the privilege of participating in the happiness God has in himself.*

---

4   Edwards, p. 62.

After all, God and his glory provide the objective ground of true happiness.[5]

As you are learning to paint, remember that you are painting a picture where joy is the overall affection you are to manifest on the canvas of your life.

From the first year of marriage—and all the years thereafter—be filled with the Spirit and paint scenes full of joy!

Questions

1. What does joy look like in your marriage?

2. What are the joy-killers lurking in your relationship?

---

5   Edwards, pp. 75-76.

CHAPTER 3

———◆———

Getting the Picture Right

'For this reason a man shall leave his father and mother and be joined to his wife, and the two shall become one flesh.' This is a great mystery, but I speak concerning Christ and the church. (Eph. 5:31-32)

First and foremost, marriage is a picture of Christ's love for His church and His church's heartfelt respect and submission to her master.

So what does your marriage picture?

You got married with expectations. You had a picture in mind. You wanted something—and you expected to get it. Now, years have passed and you may feel let down. You may have unfulfilled dreams. You never thought it would be "this way."

Your situation is not unique.

Couples get married every day for self-serving reasons. Some marry to satisfy their lust. Others crave companionship. Still others covet money or status or beauty. And more than a few are swept into marriage by a torrent of romantic feelings. Fleeting infatuation got them there.

Like most spouses, you may have come to the marriage altar with wrong motives and unrealistic ideals. But the good news is that God, through His Word, can turn it all around. God is kind. He gives a clear vision of what marriage is supposed to be. He provides a correct view so that you can frame your expectations of married life, rightly, and learn to thrive.

And what does the Bible teach? It shows us that marriage is a picture. It is a representative relationship. It *is* something on its own, but it *points* to something else. It is an earthly relationship shaped by a greater relationship that transcends it.

God designed marriage to be a living picture of love incarnate. It's meant to show forth Christ's love for the church, and the reciprocal love the church has for her Savior.

Marriage is design; it has specific contour and texture. In marriage you are painting a picture of the greatest love story ever told. I want to help you paint well by grasping the beautiful textures, colors, and depths of what marriage is as God made it.

Marriage: A Heavenly Vision Wrought by God

Marriage is God's institution. He foreordained and designed it before the world began (1 Tim. 2:9). It was a vision wrought in heaven, to be displayed on earth.

At the close of creation week, God founded the first earthly marriage when He made Adam. He formed Eve from Adam's side. He brought her to him as his wife (Gen. 2). Their union was to be fruitful as they worked together as co-stewards of God's creation (Gen. 1:28).

Husband and Wife: Representing God on Earth

In their marriage, Adam and Eve were to serve God as His image-bearers and vice-regents (Gen. 1:26-28). They were to represent God on earth.

Yet marriage's representative nature goes beyond husband and wife acting as God's earthly vice-regents; it goes to the heart of God's redemptive purpose in Christ.

Earthly marriage is meant to reflect the joys of the marriage of Christ to His church. And this representation is most fully pictured in Scripture in Ephesians 5:22-33:

Wives, submit to your own husbands, as to the Lord. For the husband is head of the wife, as also Christ is head of the church; and He is the Savior of the body. Therefore, just as the church is subject to Christ, so let the wives be to their own husbands in everything. Husbands, love your wives, just as Christ also loved the church and gave Himself for her, that He might sanctify and cleanse her with the washing of water by the word, that He might present her to Himself a glorious church, not having spot or wrinkle or any such thing, but that she should be holy and without blemish. So husbands ought to love their own wives as their own bodies; he who loves his wife loves himself. For no one ever hated his own flesh, but nourishes and cherishes it, just as the Lord does the church. For we are members of His body, of His flesh and of His bones. "For this reason a man shall leave his father and mother and be joined to his wife, and the two shall become one flesh." This is a great mystery, but I speak concerning Christ and the church. Nevertheless let each one of you in particular so love his own wife as himself, and let the wife see that she respects her husband.

"As" and "just as" are the most important words in this text. Six times we are told that marriage is to be like something.

And what is that "something"? That "something" is the most beautiful picture in the universe—Christ's love-filled marriage to His bride!

A husband represents the love of Christ—he is to sacrificially love his wife as Christ loves the church. A wife represents the submissive respect of the church toward God. A wife is to respect her earthly husband as the church respects Christ, the Eternal Bridegroom.

These comparisons are not mere metaphor; the marriage of Christ to His church is the governing archetype for earthly marriage. Though not the same at every point, Christ's redemptive marriage to His elect, which culminates in heaven (Rev. 19:6-9), pictures what marriage on earth should look like.

A Husband's Charge:
Love Your Wife as Christ Loves the Church

This means that a husband *does not represent himself* in his marriage. He represents Christ. He has a role to play. He is not his own. He cannot make up his own rules. He cannot do his own thing. Marriage is not his play-toy; it is God's institution. The painting he must emulate is illustrated in God's Word. Therefore, the husband must submit himself to the role God gave him. In this sense, he must learn how to be the man he is not. He must become like Christ. He must be faithful to the heavenly vision.

The heavenly vision is a beautiful vision of personal sacrifice. Husbands are to love their wives "just as Christ also loved the church and gave Himself for her" (Eph. 5:25).

From eternity past (2 Tim. 2:9), Christ purposed to die for His bride and save her (Matt. 1:21); and, in the due course of time, He humbly came to earth to fulfill that mission:

> *[He] made Himself of no reputation, taking the form of a bondservant, and coming in the likeness of men. And being found in appearance as a man, He humbled Himself and became obedient to the point of death, even the death of the cross. (Phil. 2:7-8)*

This is a beautiful picture. However, no man but Christ could ever love his wife as He does the church. He loves with perfect wisdom. He loves with perfect sacrifice for His beloved bride. Yet it's this picture of love that earthly husbands are called to imitate and illustrate in the pictures they paint.

The Contours of Christ's Love

Christ's love for the church is manifested in many different facets. These expressions of His love paint beautiful colors on the canvas of life, illustrating how a husband should love his wife.

In contrast to the worldly image of love, Christ shows us—with great diversity and color—what true love is.

Consider these contours of Christ's love for His church. All of these are designed to teach a husband how and what to paint:

He is present with her, *"I will never leave you nor forsake you," Heb. 13:5-6 (See also: Deut. 31:6,8; Josh. 1:5; Ps. 118:6)*

He comforts her, *"Let not your heart be troubled; you believe in God, believe also in Me. In My Father's house are many mansions," John 14:1-2*

He draws her with lovingkindness, *"The LORD has appeared of old to me, saying: 'Yes, I have loved you with an everlasting love; Therefore with lovingkindness I have drawn you,'" Jer. 31:3*

He prays for her, *"I do not pray for the world but for those whom You have given Me, for they are Yours," John 17:9 (See John 17 and Rom. 8:26)*

He is her Good Shepherd, *"I am the good shepherd. The good shepherd gives His life for the sheep," John 10:11*

He illumines her way, *"Then Jesus spoke to them again, saying, 'I am the light of the world. He who follows Me shall not walk in darkness, but have the light of life,'" John 8:12*

He nourishes her, *"holding fast to the Head, from whom all the body, nourished and knit together by joints and ligaments, grows with the increase that is from God," Col. 2:19*

He feeds her with living bread, *"I am the living bread which came down from heaven. If anyone eats of this bread, he will live forever; and the bread that I shall give is My flesh, which I shall give for the life of the world," John 6:51*

He gives living water to her, *"On the last day, that great day of the feast, Jesus stood and cried out, saying, 'If anyone thirsts, let him come to Me and drink,'" John 7:37 (See also John 4:14; Rev. 21:6)*

He eagerly desires to dine with her, *"With fervent desire I have desired to eat this Passover with you before I suffer," Luke 22:15 (See Luke 22:14-20)*

He came to seek her, *"for the Son of Man has come to seek and to save that which was lost," Luke 19:10*

He came to serve her, *"just as the Son of Man did not come to be served, but to serve, and to give His life a ransom for many," Matt. 20:28*

He finds joy in sacrificing for her, *"looking unto Jesus, the author and finisher of our faith, who for the joy that was set before Him endured the cross," Heb. 12:2 (See also Zeph. 3:17)*

He came that she might have life more abundantly, *"I have come that they may have life, and that they may have it more abundantly," John 10:10*

He made her His workmanship, *"created in Christ for good works, which God prepared beforehand," Eph. 2:10*

She is the apple of His eye, *"He kept him as the apple of His eye," Deut. 32:10*

Christ Eternally Saves, Yet Husbands Have a Rescue Mission

Husbands are called to imitate Christ's sacrificial love, yet they must recognize that only Christ can save in a redemptive sense; the work of salvation from sin is unique to Him (1 Tim. 2:5). He's the only Eternal Savior. Nonetheless, husbands should be a savior to their wives in a metaphorical sense. They ought to seek to rescue their wives in whatever ways they can as human husbands.

Specifically, a husband is "to sanctify and cleanse [his wife] with the washing of water by the word," as Christ did the church, "that He might present her to Himself a glorious church, not having spot or wrinkle or any such thing, but that she should be holy and without blemish" (Eph. 5:25-26).

The husband is not Christ, but he is to be a follower of Christ in all things. As such, husbands should draw inspiration from Christ's example as Savior:

He drank the poison cup of wrath for sin to the dregs for her, *"And He said, 'Abba, Father, all things are possible for You. Take this cup away from Me; nevertheless, not what I will, but what You will,'" Mark 14:36 (See also: Luke 22:42; Jer. 25:27-29; Ps. 75:8; Rev. 19:15)*

Christ was obedient to death for her, *"he . . . became obedient to the point of death, even the death of the cross," Phil. 2:8*

He died for her while she was ungodly, *"For when we were still without strength, in due time Christ died for the ungodly," Rom. 5:6*

Do you see how deeply Christ loves His church?

For a married man to "get the picture right," this is square one. It's a lofty and difficult assignment, yet it goes to the heart of his representative role as a husband. Day by day, Christ's sacrificial love should fill his thoughts and motivate him to be a better groom to his earthly wife. It should fuel him to greater acts of service to her. It should spawn deeper sympathy for her when she's weak and needy. It should drive him to give more and demand less, and be a shelter to his wife in the midst of life's storms.

A Wife's Charge: Submit to Your Husband, as to Christ

Just as with husbands, a wife does not represent herself in marriage. She does not make up her role. She does not manufacture her own disposition. It is a role given to her. She is a player in a drama. She does not write her own script. She is given the script that God wrote. She does not make up her lines; she is given her lines. And she is called to memorize them and speak them. There is a heavenly vision to represent.

While the central illustration of a husband's role is to love his wife as Christ loved the Church, the central picture of a wife's role is to faithfully submit to her husband, as the church is to faithfully submit to Christ:

> *Wives, submit to your own husbands, as to the Lord. For the husband is head of the wife, as also Christ is head of the church; and He is the Savior of the body. Therefore, just as the church is subject to Christ, so let the wives be to their own husbands in everything. (Eph. 5:22-24)*

A wife's pattern of submission is to mirror a faithful church.

> A faithful church is an obedient church, *"For this is the love of God, that we keep His commandments; and His commandments are not burdensome,"* 1 John 5:3 (See also Matt. 28:18-20; John 14:15; 1 John 2:3)

A faithful church is a humble church, *"Put on therefore, as the elect of God, holy and beloved, bowels of mercies, kindness, humbleness of mind,"* Col. 3:12, KJV

A faithful church is a dependent church, *"for without Me you can do nothing,"* John 15:5

A faithful church is an adoring church, *"And they sang a new song, saying: 'You are worthy to take the scroll, And to open its seals; For You were slain, And have redeemed us to God by Your blood, Out of every tribe and tongue and people and nation,'"* Rev. 5:9

A faithful church is a careful church, *"This is a faithful saying, and these things I will that thou affirm constantly, that they which have believed in God might be careful to maintain good works,"* Titus 3:8

A faithful church is full of the Spirit, *"And be not drunk with wine, wherein is excess; but be filled with the Spirit,"* Eph. 5:18, KJV

A faithful church is holy and without blemish, *"not having spot or wrinkle or any such thing,"* Eph. 5:27

A faithful church walks in the likeness of Jesus Christ, *"He who says he abides in [Christ] ought himself also to walk just as He walked,"* 1 John 2:6

A Wife's Submission:
A Living Picture of the Gospel

A wife's obedience to her husband is a type, illustration, and figure of her obedience to the Lord. She submits to Him, "as to the Lord" (Eph. 5:22). Her life pictures the church submitting to Christ. A wife's submission to her husband is an evidence that she believes the gospel and loves the Lord.

If she is not obedient to her husband, she has become a living illustration that obedience to the Lord is not necessary. This is true because true belief in the gospel leads to a life of obedience, for "faith without works is dead" (James 2:20). Scripture teaches that a wife is to "submit" to her own husband "in everything" and to "respect" him (Eph. 5:22, 24, 33). By a wife's submission she displays how the true church obeys her Lord.

God is glorified in a wife's submission. It is a picture of trust. Her trust in God is demonstrated in how she respects her husband.

Marriage: A Two-Part Harmony

Marriage is like a duet. Husband and wife sing together in two-part harmony. The words of the song are summed up in, "Jesus is Lord over whatever I feel, experience, do, and say."

In Christian marriage, you don't sing your own song. You are not singing about yourselves but, rather, about Christ and His love for the church. As a husband, you are proclaiming the message of Christ's self-sacrifice; as a wife, you are declaring the message of the church's respect and submission to Christ your husband.

You are not your own, in other words. This is not your story. You are singing a song and playing a role to please God.

What a Husband Sings

For a husband, it is the song of the gospel that God loves sinners who need to be rescued. He takes up his wife in everlasting arms, and he washes and nourishes and cherishes her. The husband is becoming like Christ. He is full of grace and truth.

If your wife is in pieces, you have commands to obey.

Women can be very delicate. Sometimes they are hard to understand. They face enormous pressure from the world. They have an emotional constitution that is generally different compared to men. God puts a man in a woman's life to love her through her seasons. There is a reason there is male leadership. There is a reason the husband is the head of the wife. There are times when a husband should lead his wife in a different direction than her emotions want to take her. There are times when she needs to be corrected. Wives need strong and holy men to lead them in the way that they should go. The need headship and the protection that headship requires.

A husband, operating like Christ, honors his wife. He serves his bride especially when she is unlovely. He only does what His Father tells him to do. He only says what His Father wants him to say. He gives himself up for her—even dying for her. He treats her tenderly as a "weaker vessel." He lives with her in an understanding way, which means that he is sensitive to her constitution, her situation, her background, and her uniqueness (1 Pet 3:7). He cares for her body, which may suffer various problems.

As a husband, you cannot do what you want to do. You cannot be who you want to be. You are bound by covenant to play a role that God created for you. It's not about you. It is not defined by you. You are only a representative—you represent Jesus Christ. You have one responsibility: whatever happens, you do what Christ would do and say what He would say.

This is the essence of true Christianity. A true Christian is a person who wants to do the will of God. A disciple is a learner and a follower of Jesus (Matt. 11:29-30). True followers of Christ deny themselves, take up their cross, and follow Jesus. Jesus said, "whoever wants to save his life will lose it" (Matt 16:25).

This means that, no matter what happens in your marriage, you will always know what to do. You have a role to play. You have a song to sing. You have lines to deliver. You have the words of Jesus Christ. Your calling is to manifest the affections of

Christ to your wife. You must have the mind of Christ for your wife. You must let the word of Christ dwell in you richly and quit speaking your own self-serving words.

When you love your wife and nourish and cherish her and wash her and prefer her in honor, you sing out a true gospel of love and pursuit. You are not distant. You are not critical. You are not dispassionate. You are not a self-absorbed groom. By the way you treat her, you are preaching a true gospel to the watching world.

What a Wife Sings

As a wife, you represent the church (Eph. 5:22-33). You are not your own. You are not on this earth to sing your own song. You are not created to make your own way. Rather, you are called to be a "glorious church, not having spot or wrinkle" (Eph. 5:27). Your motives, words, and actions are all to be governed by purity. That is why you cannot say anything you want to say. Your words must be seasoned with salt (Col. 4:6), reflecting the grace that is in your heart through the filling of the Holy Spirit.

You love and help and obey your husband. Your trust is in God's sovereign rulership of all of the people in your life. You are not frightened by any fear, because you know that God is in control. You cultivate a heart of respect toward your husband. Your beauty is in your gentle and quiet spirit.

When a wife loves, respects, helps, counsels, and submits to her husband in this way, she sings out the true gospel of the transformed life—an adoring church toward her Savior. Instead of a self-driven independent church, she is proclaiming a true gospel to her children and to the watching world.

When Marriage Proclaims a False Gospel

Here is comfort: If you understand who you are in the story, you will always know what to do. You have a role to play. You have a song to sing. You have lines to deliver. They are meant to be emanations of the Divine Being Himself.

However, if your marriage sings a different song, it portrays a false faith. Your own songs will almost always lead you into the weeds. If a husband does not love his wife and cherish her and care for her, his life preaches a false gospel. If a wife cannot say, "his banner over me [is] love" (Song of Sol. 2:4), then the husband is displaying his own glory.

If a wife is not submissive to her husband and treats him with disrespect, her life proclaims a false gospel. She is declaring that obedience to Christ does not matter, any more than obedience to her husband matters. She disobeys her husband *as to the Devil,* not *"as to the Lord"* (Eph. 5:22).

How Idolatry Shapes Marriage

When a husband and wife sing their own songs, they are worshiping themselves. They are idolaters. Idolatry is worshiping and serving the creature more than the Creator (Rom. 1:25). Idolatry is always the most problematic issue in a marriage.

Idols are never static. Wherever they loom, they will influence what we want. Whenever "having our own way" reigns, our desire to have a better marriage will simply be an outgrowth of personal selfishness. We will want more of what *we* want. Our union will be a picture of fulfilling *our* needs, conforming to *our* personality, pandering to *our* love language, coddling *our* past hurts.

When we're stuck in this rut, our marriages will be nothing more than an obsession with self: Our rights. Our wants. Our needs.

Replacing Idols with God's Vision

So why are we so often let down in our marital life? It is because what *we* wanted for our marriage all along is not what *God* wanted. Our disappointments reveal our idols and sinful passions. What we expected was simply an expression of our own selfish pride.

Not getting the point of marriage is thus very harmful. You can live for years on end, yearning for something that is an idolatrous illusion. And the sad fruit of this will be broken dreams and a broken marriage.

Yet if your expectation in marriage is that you, as a husband, learn to love your wife "just as" Christ loved the church; and you, as a wife, submit to your husband, because Christ is the head of the church, then you will get the picture right.

Your marriage will be about pointing upward to Christ rather than peering inward for self-fulfillment.

Boiling it all down, our need is really quite simple. A godly marriage seeks to earnestly embrace God's heavenly vision, not our own. Oswald Chambers writes:

> *If we lose "the heavenly vision" God has given us, we alone are responsible—not God. We lose the vision because of our own lack of spiritual growth. If we do not apply our beliefs about God to the issues of everyday life, the vision God has given us will never be fulfilled. The only way to be obedient to "the heavenly vision" is to give our utmost for His highest— our best for His glory. This can be accomplished only when we make a determination to continually remember God's vision. But the acid test is obedience to the vision in the details of our everyday life—sixty seconds out of every minute, and sixty minutes out of every hour, not just during times of personal prayer or public meetings.[1]*

---

1 Oswald Chambers, March 11 Devotional, "Obedience to the 'Heavenly Vision,'" Accessed September 15, 2023, https://utmost.org/obedience-to-the-heavenly-vision.

As you are getting the picture right, remember that you are painting a picture that mirrors the mutual love between Christ and His church. You are creating a portrait where you can see the beautiful harmony of two becoming one through scenes of mutual love and respect.

So, what if you have painted a distorted picture over the years? What if the picture you've been painting does not resemble Christ's love for the church and the church's respect for her husband?

The answer is, it is not over yet. God is a restorer. God is a healer. God blesses those who repent and go the other direction. There is hope because you still have the canvas before you. The beauty of this picture is that God has made it so that you can change the picture.

You can begin today by painting over the ugliness with His beauty.

Questions

1. What are some of the wrong expectations you came into marriage with?

2. In considering the beautiful picture of Christ and His church you are to represent, what are some specific ways you need to reform as husband and wife?

CHAPTER 4

---◆

The Aroma of Your Home

For we are to God the fragrance of Christ among those who are being saved and among those who are perishing. (2 Cor. 2:15)

A gifted painter is able to create garden scenes that can arouse even the sense of smell. In the biblical picture of marriage, there are representations and manifestations of an unseen aroma—the fragrance of Christ.

Aromas are gifts of God. They trigger memories and activate emotions. Every mother knows the pleasant sensation of the smell of her newborn. We are moved by the smell of crayons, coffee, bubblegum, leather, lavender, fresh cut grass, and cooking bacon. And then there's the sweet smell of fresh fruit—lemon, watermelon, banana, peach . . . mmm!

Your home gives off an aroma. When people walk into your house, it will have a particular aroma, a feel, an atmosphere.

When I come home from work, my wife likes to have the house smelling wonderful, so she has food cooking or an aromatic candle burning. She likes me to come in the house saying, "Mmm, this place smells good!" I'm so glad to be home!

I am glad she pays attention to the aroma of our home. But there is a different kind of aroma that cooking cannot mask. It is the aroma of love emitted by the filling of the Holy Spirit. This is the aroma of Christ.

On the other hand, a home may diffuse the relational, atmospheric equivalent of the stench of spoiled food, rotting meat, animal excrement, urine, the smell of unwashed clothes—bad breath. A home can diffuse the aroma of offenses, sour attitudes that stink. You can often detect the brimstone of toxic conversations, bad memories, and a rotting culture. It is the aroma of death.

The Doctrine

Paul tells us that the Christian filled with the Spirit gives off the aroma of death to those who are perishing and the aroma of life to those who are being saved, "For we are to God the fragrance of Christ among those who are being saved and among those who are perishing" (2 Cor. 2:15). Paul's language is rooted in the worship in the Old Testament Temple, where sacrifices were made and incense was burned, causing a pleasing aroma (Gen. 8:20-21; Lev. 23:18; Num. 28:27).

Paul taught the Corinthian church that the giving off of this aroma is not something that comes from ourselves, but from God. It is a manifestation of the work of the Holy Spirit:

> *Not that we are sufficient of ourselves to think of anything as being from ourselves, but our sufficiency is from God, who also made us sufficient as ministers of the new covenant, not of the letter but of the Spirit; for the letter kills, but the Spirit gives life. (2 Cor. 3:5-6)*

This Spirit-breathed life begins with God's saving work wherein "the love of God [is] poured out in our hearts by the Holy Spirit who was given to us" (Rom. 5:5).

The pouring out of the Spirit's love means that it is "diffused abroad," notes Adam Clarke, "filling, quickening, and invigorating all our powers and faculties."[1] Albert Barnes adds this:

> *It means here that those who are Christians shall diffuse large, and liberal, and constant blessings on their fellow-men;*

---

1   On Rom. 5:5: Albert Barnes, *Notes on the Whole Bible.*

or, as Jesus immediately explains it, that they shall be the instruments by which the Holy Spirit shall be poured down on the world.[2]

This overflow of the Spirit transfers to all of life. It's balm. It's incense. It's aura. It fills the room. It colors every corner of our walk. It enables us to carry out our duties with the fragrance of Christ (2 Cor. 2:15).

Commands Based on an Assumption

Ephesians 5:22-6:9 is part of what theologian's call, "the family life codes" or "household codes." They explain the most important assumptions and duties operating in the family life of a Christian. They are also reflected in 1 Peter 2:13-3:7, Colossians 3:18-4:1, and Titus 2:1-10. In German, they were nicknamed by Martin Luther, "Haustafeln," or "house table." They define how Christian households should be run.

In Ephesians 5:18, Paul states the foundational principle of family life—the filling of the Holy Spirit, "Do not be drunk with wine . . . but be filled with the Holy Spirit." He then develops the areas of the Spirit's power in the church (5:19-21), in the home (5:22-6:4), and in the world (6:5-20).

The filling of the Holy Spirit is the interpretive assumption in this section of Ephesians (Eph. 5:18-6:20). It is the aromatic stream through which Paul's practical directives flow. His commands to families (along with those to churches and beyond) *assume the filling of the Holy Spirit*. In other words, Paul issues the commands, assuming that they are activated and energized by the Spirit's work, "[T]he Spirit gives . . . life; the flesh profits nothing" (John 6:63).

---

2   On Rom. 5:5: Adam Clarke, *Commentary on the Whole Bible* (1831, in the public domain).

The Spirit Gives the Power to Obey

Here is the kindness of God: When He issued commands to your family, He also provided the means to accomplish those commands. He poured out His Spirit, which gives believers the unction to obey, "And I will put My Spirit within you and cause you to walk in My statutes" (Ezek. 36:27). We "love one another" (1 John 3:23) and strive to keep God's other commands because of His Spirit who dwells within us: "Now he who keeps His commandments abides in Him, and He in him. And by this we know that He abides in us, by the Spirit whom He has given us" (1 John 3:24).

However, His commands are not to be obeyed woodenly, but through diffusions of the Holy Spirit, "For it is God which works in you both to will and to do of his good pleasure" (Phil. 2:13).

The Spirit's aroma, as seen within the family, enables us to keep the commands of our respective stations:

- He commands husbands to relate to their wives with an aroma—loving, sacrificing, nourishing, cherishing, and washing (Eph. 5:25-33).

- He commands wives to relate to their husbands with an aroma—submission and respect (Eph. 5:21-24, 33).

- He commands children to relate to their parents with an aroma—honor and obedience (Eph. 6:1-3).

- He commands fathers to relate to their children with an aroma—training and admonishing them in God's ways, while not exasperating them (Eph. 6:4).

These commands for the family are not simply to be obeyed in the emptiness of sheer duty. The Holy Spirit was sent so that these duties would be filled with the flair of the fullness of God (Eph. 1:23). The astounding reality is that, when family members are filled with the Spirit, they are fountains of blessing (John 7:38; Rom. 5:5).

A Command

The command to "be filled with the Holy Spirit" (Eph. 5:18) is a *present imperative*. It indicates continuous spiritual activity in the moments of life. This means that family life is spiritual life in the "now" moments. There is an ever-flowing stream of the fullness of the life of God coursing through you as you teach, change diapers, deal with sin, and mediate conflict. It saturates vacation, work, sorrow, joy, poverty, abundance—and everything else in between. This is your life. This is how your role as a husband and a wife works. This is spiritual activity which reflects "the fragrance of Christ" (2 Cor. 2:15).

An Experience

The command to "be filled with the Holy Spirit" (Eph. 5:18) is a *present passive imperative*. There is a passivity in it; it is something that is happening to you. John the Baptist said, "a man can receive nothing unless it has been given to him from heaven" (John 3:27). In other words, God is commanding us to receive something that He enables. Even though we must take action and obey, it is not our work, but His. This means that our work is a dependent work. We are dependent upon God by the power His Holy Spirit.

A Preoccupation

A preoccupation with our Lord and Savior Jesus Christ is how families flourish. It is the way of sweetness as the aroma of the Spirit takes center stage. To be filled with the fullness of God means that you are filled with the Holy Spirit. This is manifested as you behold the face of Jesus by faith in all our duties, for "Blessed is the man who listens to me, Watching daily at my gates, Waiting at the posts of my doors. For whoever finds me finds life" (Prov. 8:34-35).

"It is the Spirit who gives life; the flesh profits nothing" (John 6:63), so we must be preoccupied with who God is if we desire life-filled marriages and homes.

Without the Spirit, Obedience Is Lifeless Rule-Keeping

Without the Spirit's power, our attempts to obey God's commands will be lifeless (John 6:63). Our homes and families will be marked by mere rule-keeping—an empty conformity and a dead orthopraxy.

In Ephesians 5:22-6:4, Paul gives clear commands to wives, husbands, children, and parents which must be obeyed, but there is a *way* in which the commands are meant to be obeyed—by the filling of the Holy Spirit (Eph. 5:18). Paul gives a moral code and the spiritual mode to carry it out. The two cannot be separated. Obedience is required duty. The Spirit is the flavor.

God designed family life to be a work of the Holy Spirit; it's an expression of the fruit of the gospel. When His moral code is uphold without the Spirit's aid, it is done in vain.

Perhaps you know nice families where this is the case. The parents want to have a good family—even a "Christian family." They teach their children to work hard, respect authority, and say "please" and "thank you." The children are expected to be obedient and polite and not to crawl over the furniture. Their parents rightly make them shake hands and look you in the eye and say, "Yes, ma'am." The children get spanked when they are wicked. They are taught to be good citizens. They have a sound moral code.

Yet their efforts are futile, for they don't have the Spirit of life. All they have are rules. In the church, these families often look like, talk like, and dress like Christian families. They know all of the Christian lingo and even enjoy Bible studies, but there is no aroma of true Christianity.

Repentance and Faith: The Path to Living Water

The truth is this—unless you are born again by the Spirit, you "cannot enter the kingdom of God" (John 3:5). Nor will you ever have the fruit of the Spirit and properly show it to your family:

> *[N]o one knows the things of God except the Spirit of God. . . . the natural man does not receive the things of the Spirit of God, for they are foolishness to him; nor can he know them, because they are spiritually discerned (1 Cor. 2:11, 14).*

If you find yourself in this position, cry out that the Spirit of God would move your heart to humbly repent of your sins and come to Christ in true faith (Acts 3:19; 1 John 1:9).

Turning to Christ in repentance is the only path to salvation (John 14:6), and it is the only way to the wellspring of the Spirit's love (Rom. 5:5)—a love that will fill your heart and overflow to others. Jesus declared, "He who believes in Me, as the Scripture has said, out of his heart will flow rivers of living water" (John 7:38).

Follow the Moral Code in Spiritual Mode

Family life is not mechanical; it is spiritual—it is life. It is designed to spring from the Spirit and be energized by the power of the Resurrection.

God calls families to an intimate connection with the Lord Jesus that compels them to love His moral code and walk in the spiritual mode, fueled by His Spirit.

In this kind of family, the parents put to death the deeds of the flesh (Rom. 8:13), while "looking unto Jesus, the author and finisher of [their] faith" (Heb. 12:2).

They recognize that rules are only meaningful by the power of the Spirit. They understand this because they believe that raising children is spiritual work. Rather than disconnecting the commands of God from the Spirit of God, they guide their family to follow Christ's ways by the sweet aroma of His Spirit.

The Fruit of the Spirit: An Aroma of Blessing

The Holy Spirit is our only hope for a blessed marriage and family, but what a bright hope the Spirit brings!

Whenever the Spirit flows, the aroma of blessing follows. The outpouring of God's Spirit fills the moments of your family life with the "fullness of Him who fills all in all" (Eph. 1:23). When this occurs, the believers in a home will attain the "stature of the fullness of Christ" (Eph. 4:13).

The filling of the Spirit is something tangible in sight and sound and smell. You can see its manifestations. It gives off the aroma of "love, joy peace patience, kindness, goodness, faithfulness, gentleness and self control" (Gal. 5:22-23)—the very fruit of the Spirit itself!

This fruit should flow throughout your home and family life, sweetening every interaction:

- Love: You show patient and sacrificial love
- Joy: Your face reflects the joy of your heart
- Peace: You are a peaceful presence
- Patience: You speak and act out of patience
- Kindness: You have a generous spirit
- Goodness: You draw one another into goodness
- Faithfulness: You keep at it in the face of resistance
- Gentleness: You offer counsel in a spirit of gentleness
- Self-Control: You respond to conflict with self-control

Be Filled with the Fragrance of Christ

When the fruit of Spirit flows through you, your family will be transformed. Your home will literally be delivered out of your own smelly ways into the pleasantly aromatic ways of God (2 Cor. 2:15).

So what is the application?

Make sure your family is not simply about rules. There are the things you should and *must* do, but there is only *one way* they should be done—through the filling of the Holy Spirit (Eph. 5:18).

Even as lifeless rule-keeping should be avoided, don't go to the other extreme and be afraid of laws and commands. The Spirit bears witness of the ways of God (1 Cor. 2:12) which we're to willingly follow: "For this is the love of God, that we keep His commandments. And His commandments are not burdensome" (1 John 5:3).

As you seek the glory of God, let your home be marked by law and grace, truth and love, Word and Spirit.

As you are getting the picture right, learn how to illustrate compelling scenes that arouse a sense of the aroma of the Holy Spirit. Let all of family life be filled with the "fragrance of Christ" (2 Cor. 2:15)—the best kind of aromatherapy there is.

Questions

1. How would you describe the "feel" or the "aroma" of your house when your family is at home?

2. What are the *right things* that you are doing in the *wrong way?*

CHAPTER 5

Making Christ the Center of Your Marriage

And He is before all things, and in Him all things consist. And He is the head of the body, the church, who is the beginning, the firstborn from the dead, that in all things He may have the preeminence. (Col. 1:17-18)

In the biblical picture of marriage, Christ is at the center.

We start with this proposition: Christ is head of His church and head over all things, as Paul declared to the Colossians (Col. 1:17-18). In the NASB's rendering of this text, the word "preeminence" is translated as the "first place in everything." He is thus preeminent over marriage.

Jonathan Edwards describes how beneficial it is to manifest the glory of Christ in the world:

> *When the creature displays excellent qualities and happiness, it is nothing more than the expressions of God's glory shining in and through them. Thus, in seeking their glory and happiness, God makes himself his own ultimate end (that is, himself diffused and shining outwardly, which he delights in just as he delights in his innate beauty and fullness), he seeks their glory and happiness as well.[1]*

So how do we bear out this truth in practice?

The first thing we must acknowledge is that Christ's preeminence over marriage, and all other things, exists whether

---

1   Edwards, p. 109.

we recognize it or not. His position of supreme rank and authority doesn't rise or fall with our opinions; it simply is because of who He is as God.

Square One: Be Born Again Followers of Christ

Yet to properly recognize Him as our preeminent Lord, we must first be followers of Jesus Christ. You cannot make Christ the center of your marriage until Christ is first in your heart.

So where are you on this spectrum? Have you repented of your sins? Have you renounced the world and its counterfeits? Have you received the gift of the Holy Spirit? Has the power of sin been broken? Have your affections changed from loving darkness to loving the light?

According to Jesus, being born again, a work wrought by the Spirit, is step one in this process:

> *Most assuredly, I say to you, unless one is born again, he cannot see the kingdom of God. . . . unless one is born of water and the Spirit, he cannot enter the kingdom of God. That which is born of the flesh is flesh, and that which is born of the Spirit is spirit. Do not marvel that I said to you, 'You must be born again.' The wind blows where it wishes, and you hear the sound of it, but cannot tell where it comes from and where it goes. So is everyone who is born of the Spirit. (John 3:3, 5-8)*

When we are born of the Spirit, we enter into Christ's kingdom. This comes by humbly believing in Him as the author of our salvation:

> *For God so loved the world that He gave His only begotten Son, that whoever believes in Him should not perish but have everlasting life. For God did not send His Son into the world to condemn the world, but that the world through Him might*

be saved. He who believes in Him is not condemned; but he who does not believe is condemned already, because he has not believed in the name of the only begotten Son of God. And this is the condemnation, that the light has come into the world, and men loved darkness rather than light, because their deeds were evil. For everyone practicing evil hates the light and does not come to the light, lest his deeds should be exposed. But he who does the truth comes to the light, that his deeds may be clearly seen, that they have been done in God. (John 3:16-21)

By bowing the knee to Christ in faith, and trusting Him to save us, we place Him at the very center of our lives. We declare Him to be the preeminent God He is.

The Core Question: What Is Pleasing to Christ in Everything?

Once this matter of salvation is resolved, the main question a couple should ask is this: "In every choice we make in our marriage, what is pleasing to our Lord Jesus Christ?"

What is pleasing to Christ in our conversations, friends, discipline of children, handling money, church life, changing jobs, vacations, daily schedule, relocating? What is pleasing to Him in the music we listen to? What is pleasing to Him in the films we watch? What is pleasing to Him in our sexual life?

What is pleasing to Him in everything!

This is the essence of making Christ the center of your marriage. As the "only wise God" (Jude 25, KJV), He is to:

- Be the most important person in your marriage
- Be the curator of your wedded life
- Be the greatest influence
- Be the dominating presence
- Be the supreme authority

- Be the prism through which everything is seen
- Be the fountainhead of wisdom
- Be your nourishment as living bread
- Be your refreshment as living water
- Be the first place in everything
- Have the best seat in all discussions
- Have the last and final word

To make Christ preeminent requires self-denial:

> *Jesus said to His disciples, "If anyone desires to come after Me, let him deny himself, and take up his cross, and follow Me. For whoever desires to save his life will lose it, but whoever loses his life for My sake will find it. For what profit is it to a man if he gains the whole world, and loses his own soul? Or what will a man give in exchange for his soul?" (Matt. 16:24-26)*

It calls for sold-out service to Him:

> *He who loves his life will lose it, and he who hates his life in this world will keep it for eternal life. If anyone serves Me, let him follow Me; and where I am, there My servant will be also. If anyone serves Me, him My Father will honor. (John 12:25-26)*

A Four-Way Pact to Make Christ Preeminent

In pursuing this end, here's a helpful four-way pact to make Christ preeminent in your marriage.

First, devote yourselves to His preeminence.

Take a step, together as a couple, to self-consciously establish the headship of Christ as the centerpiece of your marriage. Declare that He will and must have the pre-eminence, "And He is the head of the body, the church, who is the beginning, the firstborn from the dead, that in all things He may have the preeminence" (Col. 1:18).

Make Jesus Christ the sole influencer and arbiter in everything.

Second, count all things as loss for the sake of Christ.

Note Paul's declaration:

> *But what things were gain to me, these I have counted loss for Christ. Yet indeed I also count all things loss for the excellence of the knowledge of Christ Jesus my Lord, for whom I have suffered the loss of all things, and count them as rubbish, that I may gain Christ. (Phil. 3:7-8)*

In this statement to the Philippians, Paul is addressing worldly accomplishments. He counts them all as loss compared to Christ. Temporal accolades are "rubbish" to him.

Marriages often fall on the sword of ambition or the pursuit of some vain accomplishment. As a couple, it is imperative that you let nothing get in the way of applying the wisdom and knowledge of Christ to every endeavor, "Let us pursue the knowledge of the Lord" (Hosea 6:3), "in whom are hidden all the treasures of wisdom and knowledge" (Col. 2:3).

All other pursuits are folly.

Third, behold the glory of Christ.

> *But we all, with unveiled face, beholding as in a mirror the glory of the Lord, are being transformed into the same image from glory to glory, just as by the Spirit of the Lord. (2 Cor. 3:18)*

Beholding Christ's glory transforms us into His image.

His splendor gives us strength. Christ at the center of your marriage is the means not only of your justification, but also of our sanctification. We need "the help of His countenance" to thrive (Ps. 42:5).

Beholding Christ foments the changes that we need. Over time, our thinking is purified, and our affections are modified for the good.

Beholding Christ's glory increases faith. It quickens joy and fills our souls with light.

The light of Christ's countenance is what led the children of Israel to victory in the Promised Land, and it can propel us to victory also, "But it was Your right hand, Your arm, and the light of Your countenance, because You favored them" (Ps. 44:3).

It is the key to blessing:

The Lord bless you and keep you; The Lord make His face shine upon you and be gracious to you; the Lord lift up His countenance upon you, and give you peace. (Num. 6:24-26)

So many of the things that sweeten marriage are found in the countenance of Jesus Christ:

Lord, lift up the light of Your countenance upon us.
You have put gladness in my heart,
More than in the season that their grain and wine increased.
I will both lie down in peace, and sleep;
For You alone, O Lord, make me dwell in safety. (Ps. 4:6-8)

As couples, we should earnestly cry out to God to visit us with His presence, "Seek the Lord while He may be found, call upon Him while He is near" (Isa. 55:6).

The good news is this: When we seek the glory of Christ's countenance with our whole hearts, He will show it to us, "And you will seek Me and find Me, when you search for Me with all your heart. I will be found by you, says the Lord" (Jer. 29:13).

Simply put, the glory of Christ's presence is the greatest strength of a marriage.

Jonathan Edwards explains it this way:

It works like this: God delights in his inner, innate glory, but he also delights equally in the shining emanation of his glory.

The overflowing phase of his glory is how he communicates his excellent qualities to the creature, and this is the source of their happiness. Therefore, in the one act of shining forth his glory, God both honors himself and makes his people happy and joyful. His desire to glorify himself and his desire to bring good to his creatures are not at odds.[2]

Fourth, set your minds on the truth.

The entertainment industry can have a corrosive effect on your marriage in so many ways. With this in mind, saturate your home with what is true and beautiful, and deprive it of what dulls your love for the Lord:

Finally, brethren, whatever things are true, whatever things are noble, whatever things are just, whatever things are pure, whatever things are lovely, whatever things are of good report, if there is any virtue and if there is anything praiseworthy—meditate on these things. The things which you learned and received and heard and saw in me, these do, and the God of peace will be with you. (Phil. 4:8-9)

When Christ Is Preeminent in Marriage, Blessings Flow

When Christ is the center of your wedded life, blessings will flow throughout every facet of your marriage experience.

J.R. Miller captured this in his book, *Secrets of a Happy Home Life*:

What are some of the secrets of happy home life?
The answer might be given in one word—Christ.
Christ at the marriage-altar;
Christ on the bridal journey;

---

2 Edwards, p. 109.

Christ when the new home is set up;
Christ when the baby is born;
Christ when a child dies;
Christ in the pinching times;
Christ in the days of plenty;
Christ in the nursery, in the kitchen, in the parlor;
Christ in the toil and in the rest;
Christ along all the years;
Christ when the wedded pair walk toward the sunset gates;
Christ in the sad hour when farewells are spoken, and one goes on before and the other stays, bearing the unshared grief;
Christ is the secret of a happy home life.[3]

To get the picture right, remember that Christ must be at the center of everything you are painting.

Questions

1. Have you been born again? Do you believe that Jesus Christ is the Savior? Are you trusting in the righteousness of Christ through His substitutionary death and showing evidence that the power of sin has been broken? Has your life changed as a result?

2. Have you resolved to make Christ the prism through which you see everything in your marriage?

3   J.R. Miller, *Secrets of a Happy Home Life* (New York: Thomas Y. Crowell & Company, 1894), pp. 6-7.

CHAPTER 6

———————➤

Authority and Submission

Wives, submit to your own husbands, as to the Lord. For the husband is head of the wife, as also Christ is head of the church; and He is the Savior of the body. Therefore, just as the church is subject to Christ, so let the wives be to their own husbands in everything. (Eph. 5:22-24)

The biblical picture of marriage includes authority and submission.

The happiest and most stately women I've ever known are submissive women. They know who they are. They know what to do. They understand how to integrate themselves into God's order of things. They are the most confident. They are the most at peace. They are the most unflappable. They fear no man. They are content. They walk in the old paths. They are on the highway of holiness.

I was struck by something former lesbian activist Rosaria Butterfield said after she encountered such Christian women when she was invited to a pastor's home for a meal. This encounter shook her and was used by God in bringing her to Christ, "The calmness of the women was serene and strange. No grandstanding. No holding court. No gossip. These were old friends with deep connections who knew how to belly laugh."[1]

---

1 Rosaria Butterfield, *Five Lies of Our Anti-Christian Age* (Wheaton, IL: Crossway, 2023), pp. 259-260. Kindle Edition.

In contrast, there are the fitful, grasping, unfulfilled, and insecure women who have not humbled themselves under God's authority. They tend to be unhappy, and they have their medications to prove it.

A Wife's Submission: The Biblical Parameters

God calls wives to be submissive to their husbands, and He explains the details.

First, the word "submissive" unequivocally explains the meaning. The word used here is a military term, indicating order and authority.[2] It has nothing to do with superiority; rather, order and authority. The husband has the higher rank.

Second, to whom is a wife to be submissive? To her "own" husband (Eph. 5:22; 1 Pet. 3:1)—not every man!

Third, how is she to be submissive?—"as unto the Lord" (Eph. 5:22, KJV).

A wife submits to her husband in the same spirit as she does to the Lord. As the Lord is preeminent, so is her husband preeminent in her life, second only to Christ. Christ is the head of the church, and the husband is the head of the wife. This is one reason a woman should be very careful whom she marries.

Fourth, when is she supposed to be submissive? The context is very broad. It is a submission "in everything" (Eph. 5:24). This does not mean she must submit to her husband in what is immoral, illegal, or unlawful before the Lord.

Women will have a tendency to think that their duty of submission makes them slaves to their husbands. However, we must remember that the husband is under divine obligation to be

---

2 *hupotasso* (G5293 in Strong's); *Vine's Expository Dictionary of New Testament Word*: hupotasso is "primarily a military term, 'to rank under' (hupo, 'under,' tasso, 'to arrange'); Strong's: "to subordinate; reflexively, to obey:—be under obedience (obedient), put under, subdue unto, (be, make) subject (to, unto), be (put) in subjection (to, under), submit self unto."

good to his wife by loving her in a very special way—"as Christ also loved the church and gave himself up for her" (Eph. 5:25).

A Husband's Authority: Biblical Proofs

Here are some of Scripture's key proofs of a husband's authority:

1. God is the one who appoints all authorities (Rom. 13:1).

2. The titles of a husband place him in higher authority: "lord" (1 Pet. 3:6); "head"(1 Cor. 11:3); and "image and glory of God" (1 Cor. 11:7).

3. The position the husband holds represents Christ, and the wife's position represents a submissive church (Eph. 5:23).

4. The woman was created for man (Gen. 2:18-24; 1 Cor. 11:8-9).

5. The wife does not have authority over her husband because, "Adam was formed first, then Eve. And Adam was not deceived, but the woman being deceived, fell into transgression" (1 Tim. 2:13-14).[3]

On the other hand, you have men who are real leaders in their homes. Husbands who are becoming like Christ are true patriarchs. They practice "father rule," the definition of a patriarch.[4] They work out their patriarchy the way the Bible describes it (Eph. 5:22-33; 1 Pet. 3:1-7). They are being transformed into the likeness of Christ. The kind of patriarchy I'm for is Christlike patriarchy.

These patriarchs understand God has given them authority. It's real authority. It's accountable authority. It is the kind of authority women need. God gives husbands the power to say "yes" and "no" (Num. 30).

---

3 These proofs are adapted from William Gouge, *Building a Godly Home: A Holy Vision for a Happy Marriage*, Chapter 8, "A Wife's Respect for Her Husband" (Grand Rapids, MI: Reformation Heritage Books, 2013), pp. 98-117.

4 For more on the history of the word patriarch, see: patriarch (*n.*). https://www.etymonline.com/word/patriarch.

My experience as a pastor is that when you have men who have embraced their responsibility to lead, you have a lot less marriage counseling to do. Wives are better adjusted. They have humbled themselves. These husbands are taking care of their wives. They are leading. They are patriarchs after the pattern of Jesus Christ.

God's glory shines as husbands and wives publicly display authority and submission in marriage:

> ... people who love the sun's appearance, and see it as an amiable and glorious thing, want it to shine brightly, diffusing and spreading its glory throughout the whole world. They do not want its glory to be contained or trapped.[5]

A Wife's Place: Lower in Rank, But Superior on Many Fronts

The Bible does not teach that the husband and wife are of equal rank and authority. This is difficult for most women to swallow. They know that they are as good as their husbands and maybe better. They may be smarter. They may be wiser. They may be more theologically adept.

William Gouge illustrates:

> Though the man be as the head, yet the woman is as the heart, which is the most excellent part of the body beside the head, far more excellent than any other member under the head, and almost equal to the head in many respects, and as necessary as the head. As an evidence that a wife is to the man as the heart to the head.[6]

Still, someone must have the final decision, and God has given this role to the husband. However, every man must recognize

5   Edwards, p. 96.
6   Gouge, p. 102.

that God gave him a wife to counsel him, to talk to him. He is required to listen to her because he loves her. She is his "helper." And, he needs help! With this recognized, we should be reminded of the saying, "Every well-functioning head has two ears." Wise husbands recognize their need for the intellectual capacity, wise counsel, and foresight of their wives.

God calls a wife into a disposition of respect, "Let the wife see that she respects her husband" (Eph. 5:33). This is a very deep respect for the position, as a wife is called to relate to her husband as her "lord" (1 Pet. 3:6).

How should a wife relate to a disobedient husband? 1 Peter 3:1-4 makes it clear that she wins "without a word" through a "gentle and quiet spirit." She wins him through her respect and love, not her words or her war against him.

Women often misunderstand how to win a man. Most men are not able to hear if there is too much heat. It is both a weakness and a strength of manhood.

William Gouge puts it this way:

> *Let wives therefore learn first to moderate their passion, and then to keep in their tongues with bit and bridle, but most of all to be careful that their husbands do not taste the bitterness of it, even if they should be provoked by some oversight of their husband's.*[7]

When her husband is sinning, the wife should refrain from continuously repeating his faults, lest she become a contentious wife with a constant dripping that makes a husband prefer living on the corner of the roof (Prov. 19:13; 21:9,19; 25:24; 27:15).

---

7 Gouge, p. 116.

To Husbands and Wives: Honor God's Boundaries with Respect and Love

If a wife cannot willingly order herself under her husband's authority, she will be tempted to heartlessly submit. She will bitterly submit to her spouse as a conqueror, but it will only embitter her until she casts herself on the mercy of God and yields to the will of the Lord who made her.

Authority without love is tyranny. The husband who orders his wife around and forces her to submit does not understand that a wife's submission is not forced submission, but voluntary submission. This is the language of the text, "Wives, submit to your own husbands" (Eph. 5:22).

The Bible never teaches husbands to force their wives to submit. It is a horrible tragedy when you have a husband who is not loving his wife like Christ loves the church. It is heartbreaking when a husband is not submissive to our Lord Jesus Christ. It makes it hard for wives to thrive.

It is quite possible for husbands to make wives sin through sinful use of authority, in the same way a father can cause his children to sin by exasperating and discouraging them (Eph. 6:1-4; Col. 3:21). It is very sad when a good woman is saddled with a corrupt husband, as Solomon implied, "Woe to you, O land, when your king is a child, And your princes feast in the morning!" (Eccl. 10:16).

This is why the authority of a husband, under our Lord's authority, is always seasoned with love (Eph. 5:25). Gouge states:

Because as Christ by showing first His love stirs up the church to love Him, so a husband by loving his wife should stir up her to love him in return. Showing himself like the sun which is the fountain of light, and from which the moon receives what light she has, so he should be the fountain of love to his wife.[8]

---

8   Gouge, p. 182.

Upholding God's Order: Husbands and Wives Must Play Their Roles

These duties of authority and submission, respect and love, are the mutual duties of a husband and a wife. God has called husbands and wives to play their roles.

All of these roles are designed to operate under the influence of the Holy Spirit: "do not be drunk with wine . . . but be filled with the Holy Spirit" (Eph. 5:18); "But the fruit of the Spirit is love, joy, peace, longsuffering, kindness, goodness, faithfulness, gentleness, self-control. Against such there is no law" (Gal. 5:22-23).

As you are learning to paint pictures of Christ's love for His church, learn how to represent the free-flowing interplay of the mutual duties of a husband and a wife.

These duties are not bondage! They set people free to be what they were meant to be under the influence of the Holy Spirit.

Questions

1. As a husband, are you exercising godly authority over your wife, and are there areas of passivity that need to be addressed?

2. As a wife, are you happily exercising faithful submission, or are you kicking against it as a bondage?

CHAPTER 7

---------◆

Don't Be Hard to Live With

For all the law is fulfilled in one word, even in this: "You shall love your neighbor as yourself." But if you bite and devour one another, beware lest you be consumed by one another! I say then: Walk in the Spirit, and you shall not fulfill the lust of the flesh. (Gal. 5:14-16)

As you learn to paint, remember that you are painting scenes of the lives of two people—two who have become one. In the biblical picture of marriage you find an uncommon union where life is not hard. Rather it is easy when you walk in the Spirit (Gal. 5:22-25).

What is it like to live with you? Have you made it hard or easy on your spouse?

Know that your actions are never static—they will always bear fruit. How you treat your mate will either promote their wellbeing or wear them down.

Think of it like fabrics. Some are scratchy and irritating, while others are smooth and soothing. So it is with spouses. You can lift them up or make life hard for them.

It's a bit like roads and cars. Some roads are harder on cars than others. They cause more wear and tear. If you live in a place where they salt the roads during winter, within a few years, your car body will rust. And if the conditions are really harsh, the frame will decay so badly over time that you'll have to get rid of it as a safety hazard.

Bad relationship conditions will always take their toll, and you can see it on the face of the beleaguered.

If you're mired in relationship challenges, the years can miserably wear on you—especially when you're married to someone who's hard to live with. And if you're the offending culprit, your partner will bear the scars.

Hard to Live With: Men and Women in the Bible

The Bible shows us both men and women who fit this mold.

Solomon describes how a woman like this will grate on those around her, "A continual dripping on a very rainy day and a contentious woman are alike" (Prov. 27:15), adding this: "Better to dwell in the wilderness than with a contentious and angry woman" (Prov. 21:19).

Then there is Nabal. He impudently "reviled" messengers of David when they sought his help (1 Sam. 25:14). Nabal was so "harsh and badly behaved" as a husband (1 Sam. 25:2, ESV) that his wife Abigail dared not consult with him when she intervened with David to deescalate tensions—tensions that Nabal had needlessly caused through his rash insults (1 Sam. 25:19).

And the examples continue:

- **Adam was hard to live with**. Rather than take responsibility for his sin, he blamed his wife Eve for the Fall (Gen. 3:11-12).

- **Job's wife was hard to live with**. In response to Job's piety, she condemned him saying, "Curse God and die" (Job 2:9).

- **Abraham was hard to live with**. He twice put his wife's virtue in jeopardy to save his own life (Gen. 12:10-20; 20:1-13).

- **Rachel was hard to live with**. Being envious of her sister's fruitfulness, she complained to her husband, "Give me children, or else I die" (Gen. 30:1-2).

- **Moses' wife was hard to live with.** She angrily circumcised their son, threw the foreskin at his feet, and bristled, "[Y]ou are a bridegroom of blood to me" (Ex. 4:25, ESV)
- **Gomer was hard to live with.** Despite her husband's unfailing love, she repeatedly acted as a harlot (Hos. 1-3).

Fourteen Foul Vices

While not an exhaustive list, here are fourteen foul vices that will make you hard to live with. Left to your flesh, you can easily be:

- Prideful and narcissistic (James 4:6, Ps. 75:4; 1 John 2:16; Prov. 25:27; 2 Tim. 3:1-9)
- Impatient (Prov. 15:18; 29:20; 1 Cor. 13:4)
- Discontented (Prov. 27:20; Eccles. 5:10; Gen. 30:1-2)
- Unloving (Rom. 1:31; 2 Tim. 3:3)
- Unforgiving (Rom. 1:31; 2 Tim. 3:3)
- Unmerciful (Rom. 1:31; Matt. 18:23-35)
- Unkind (Eph. 4:29; Col. 3:12)
- Unfaithful (Prov. 25:19; Matt. 5:27-28)
- Prone to unfiltered speech (Prov. 13:3; 15:28; 29:11)
- Inclined to rash and quick responses (Prov. 12:18; 29:20; James 1:19)
- Given to harsh words (Prov. 15:1; 1 Sam. 25:1-11)
- Bitter (Eph. 4:31-32; Heb. 12:15; James 3:14-16)
- Angry (Eph. 4:31-32; James 1:19-20)
- Selfish (Phil. 2:3; 1 Cor. 10:24; 1 Cor. 13:4-5)

Fighting the War Within: The Spirit vs. the Flesh

Christians aren't exempt from falling into one or more of these vile sins. With this in view, Paul commands that we are to "no longer walk as" an unbeliever (Eph. 4:17). We are to "put off, concerning your former conduct, the old man which grows corrupt according to the deceitful lusts, and be renewed in the spirit of your mind, and that you put on the new man which was created according to God, in true righteousness and holiness" (Eph. 4:22-24).

He then gives these specifics:

> *Let no corrupt word proceed out of your mouth, but what is good for necessary edification, that it may impart grace to the hearers. And do not grieve the Holy Spirit of God, by whom you were sealed for the day of redemption. Let all bitterness, wrath, anger, clamor, and evil speaking be put away from you, with all malice. And be kind to one another, tenderhearted, forgiving one another, just as God in Christ forgave you. (Eph. 4:29-32)*

Paul contrasts the deeds of the old and new man, while emphasizing the indwelling of the Holy Spirit who mourns when we yield to the flesh. Matthew Henry writes, "it is intimated that those corrupt passions of bitterness, and wrath, and anger, and clamour, and evil speaking, and malice, grieve this good Spirit."[1]

The good news for the Christian is that the Holy Spirit not only serves as our conscience when we treat others wrongly, but it gives us the power to forsake sin and treat others the right way:

> *But if you bite and devour one another, beware lest you be consumed by one another! I say then: Walk in the Spirit, and you shall not fulfill the lust of the flesh. For the flesh lusts*

---

1   On Eph. 4:17-32: Matthew Henry, *Commentary on the Whole Bible* (1811).

against the Spirit, and the Spirit against the flesh; and these are contrary to one another. (Gal. 5:15-17)

Paul writes in Romans of this ongoing war. Even though our inward man has been renewed, there remains "another law in [our] members, warring against the law of [our] mind" (Rom. 7:23). Yet because our "old man was crucified with" Christ, "we should no longer be slaves of sin. . . . therefore do not let sin reign in your mortal body, that you should obey it in its lusts" (Rom. 6:6, 12).

"A Christian," writes John Piper, "is not a person who experiences no bad desires. A Christian is a person who is at war with those desires by the power of the Spirit."[2]

The bottom line is this: If you yield to your flesh, you will be hard to live with and be a grief to your spouse and children and church, but if you war against it by walking in the Spirit, you will be an encouraging blessing, for:

[T]he fruit of the Spirit is love, joy, peace, long-suffering, gentleness, goodness, faith, Meekness, temperance: against such there is no law. And they that are Christ's have crucified the flesh with the affections and lusts. If we live in the Spirit, let us also walk in the Spirit. (Gal. 5:22-25)

How to Walk in the Spirit

So how, practically speaking, are we to "walk in the Spirit" (Gal. 5:25) and be "filled with the Spirit," as Paul stressed (Eph. 5:18)?

Pursue Holiness

First, to walk in the Spirit it is to pursue holiness. This is how we put on the new man.

---

2   John Piper, "The War Within: Flesh Versus Spirit," *Desiring God* (blog), June 19, 1983. Accessed July, 20, 2023, https://www.desiringgod.org/messages/the-war-within-flesh-versus-spirit.

Paul writes, "put on the new man which was created according to God, in true righteousness and holiness" (Eph. 4:24).

Peter affirms this, writing that "as obedient children," do not conform "yourselves to the former lusts, as in your ignorance; but as He who called you is holy, you also be holy in all your conduct, because it is written, 'Be holy, for I am holy'" (1 Pet. 1:14-16).

Deep down, we should fervently long for holiness. And when we fail to do so, we will easily fall prey to the flesh.

Be Filled with God's Word

Second, to be filled with the Spirit is to be filled with God's Word.

Jesus declared, "But the Helper, the Holy Spirit, whom the Father will send in My name, He will teach you all things, and bring to your remembrance all things that I said to you" (John 14:26). Jesus added that the Spirit is truth itself who will testify of it: "the Spirit of truth who proceeds from the Father, He will testify of Me" (John 15:26); "when He, the Spirit of truth, has come, He will guide you into all truth" (John 16:13).

For the Holy Spirit to "bring to [our] remembrance all things" that Christ said (John 14:26), we must know what He said first. We should therefore be diligent students of God's Word and long to obey it. Our heart should reflect that of the psalmist, "With my whole heart have I sought you: Oh let me not wander from your commandments. Your word have I hidden in my heart, that I might not sin against You" (Ps. 119:10-11).

"Let the word of Christ dwell in you richly in all wisdom," wrote Paul (Col. 3:16). When we treasure God's Word in our heart, the Holy Spirit will bring it to mind when we're tempted to mistreat others and spur us to right behavior instead (John 14:26).

Walk in Obedience

Third, to be filled with the Spirit is to walk in obedience to God.

Paul's command to obedience is direct: "do not let sin reign in your mortal body, that you should obey it in its lusts" (Rom. 6:12).

So is Peter's. As quoted above, he writes that, "as obedient children," do not conform "yourselves to the former lusts" (1 Pet. 1:14), but rather obey "the truth through the Spirit in sincere love" (1 Pet. 1:22). Peter later states that to godliness we are to add:

> . . . *brotherly kindness, and to brotherly kindness love. For if these things are yours and abound, you will be neither barren nor unfruitful in the knowledge of our Lord Jesus Christ. For he who lacks these things is shortsighted, even to blindness, and has forgotten that he was cleansed from his old sins. Therefore, brethren, be even more diligent to make your call and election sure, for if you do these things you will never stumble; . . . Beloved, I beg you as sojourners and pilgrims, abstain from fleshly lusts which war against the soul. (2 Pet. 1:7-10; 1 Pet. 2:11)*

Just as in Paul's writings, Peter showcases the fierce war between the flesh and the spirit, while giving an earnest call to obedience. We are to diligently fight our sinful lusts, even as we show forth brotherly kindness and love.

This is how we walk in the Spirit and become a blessing to our spouse.

An Uncommon Union: Jonathan and Sarah Edwards

Couples who get it right enjoy happy marriages.

Consider the remarkable example of Jonathan and Sarah Edwards. Some have viewed Edwards as a difficult man. But the eyewitnesses who observed his relationship to his wife Sarah tell a different story—that the two experienced a rich and blessed marriage together.

Elizabeth Dodds, the great biographer of this couple's life, writes:

> *The real Jonathan Edwards, the man, the person, was a tender husband, an effective and affectionate father, a human being quite unlike the image of him as the stern preacher of sermons about sin. His happy marriage to Sarah Pierrepont was more than a loving link between two people: it was Edwards' link to life—to the practical; to warm fireplaces, good food, attractive surroundings; to devotion, to the dailyness of the Incarnation. What Edwards described as their 'uncommon union' bonded them marvelously to one another and it also bonded them to the living God.[3]*

Not only was Jonathan tender and affectionate, but Sarah "did all as the service of love, and so doing it with a continual, uninterrupted cheerfulness, peace and joy."[4]

Samuel Hopkins, a young man in his twenties who lived eight months in the Edwards home, wrote this of her:

> *While she uniformly paid a becoming deference to her husband and treated him with entire respect, she spared no pains in conforming to his inclination and rendering everything in the family agreeable and pleasant; accounting it her greatest glory and there wherein she could best serve God and her generation, to be the means in this way of promoting his usefulness and happiness.[5]*

Hopkins was taken by the way they treated one another, remarking that "no person of discernment could be conversant in the family without observing and admiring the perfect harmony and mutual love and esteem that subsisted between them."[6]

---

3   Elisabeth S. Dodds, "My Dear Companion," Christian History, Issue 8 (1985).
4   *Ibid.*
5   Elisabeth D. Dodds, *Marriage to a Difficult Man: The 'Uncommon Union' of Jonathan and Sarah Edwards* (Philadelphia: The Westminster Press, 1971), p. 35.
6   *Ibid.*, p. 26.

On his deathbed, Jonathan was separated from Sarah. He had been hired as president of Princeton University and moved there to get settled, with his family to follow later. He took the smallpox vaccine and fell dangerously ill. In his dying moments he whispered to his daughter Lucy:

> *It seems to me to be the will of God, that I must shortly leave you; therefore give my kindest love to my dear wife, and tell her, that the uncommon union, which has so long subsisted between us, has been of such a nature, as I trust is spiritual, and therefore will continue for ever: and I hope she will be supported under so great a trial, and submit cheerfully to the will of God.*[7]

When Sarah learned of her husband's death, she praised God for their marriage in a letter:

> *He has made me adore his goodness that we had him so long. . . . O what a legacy my husband, and your father, has left to us! We are all given to God; and there I am, and love to be. Your ever affectionate mother, Sarah Edwards*[8]

Conclusion

Is your marriage an uncommon union? Is your relationship with your mate characterized by such poignant tenderness?

Or are you hard to live with instead?

If the latter is true, you need to understand that you can embitter your spouse by your ill behavior.

Repeated stress can lead to a breaking point, as in Mean Time to Failure (MTTF).[9] This is an engineering term that is used to determine when a product, material, or machine will break down as a result of repeated use. For example, how many

7   Sereno E. Dwight, "Memoirs of Jonathan Edwards," in *Works*, 1:clxxviii.
8   *Ibid.*, 1:clxxix.
9   Jonathan Davis, "What Is Mean Time to Failure?" *Hippocmms* (blog), March 24, 2021. Accessed July 20, 2023, https://hippocmms.iofficecorp.com/blog/what-is-mean-time-to-failures-mttf.

flips of a light switch or miles on a set of brake pads will it take before they fail?

Rather than having a "total system failure" in your marriage, resolve to repent and become easy to live with by walking in the Spirit.

Be patient with your spouse. Thoughtfully listen to one another. Respond to each other's needs and concerns in Christian charity. Prefer one another in honor. Be a loving companion who can freely state, "This is my beloved, and this is my friend" (Song of Sol. 5:16).

Make it your aim to put off the old man, even as you "put on tender mercies, kindness, humility, meekness, longsuffering; bearing with one another, and forgiving one another, if anyone has a complaint against another; even as Christ forgave you, so you also must do" (Col. 3:12-13).

Your choice is simple—cave to the flesh or live by the spirit. And know that your marriage will be shaped—in kind, "For to be carnally minded is death, but to be spiritually minded is life and peace" (Rom. 8:6).

As you are getting the picture right, learn how to paint the picture of ease and contentment that comes when you walk in the Spirit—don't be hard to live with!

Rather than be a constantly dripping wife (Prov. 27:15) or a "harsh and badly behaved" husband (1 Sam. 25:3, ESV), follow the Spirit's lead in your marriage and find true peace.

Questions

1. If you are hard to live with, what are you doing that makes it hard?

2. If you are living with someone who is hard to live with, what should you do about it in obedience to the commands of God?

CHAPTER 8

How to Correct Your Spouse

[H]e who has clean hands shall be stronger and stronger.
(Job 17:9)

In the biblical picture of marriage you find mutual cleansing. This is the washing of water by the Word through the ordinary interactions of life.

One of the beautiful pictures of marriage is a husband washing his wife. As a result of his life with her, she is progressively cleansed (Eph. 5:26).

God uses washing as a picture to convey the beauty of salvation:

When the Lord has washed away the filth of the daughters of Zion . . . there will be a tabernacle for shade in the daytime from the heat, for a place of refuge, and for a shelter from storm and rain. (Isa. 4:4,6)

For life to flourish, filth must be cleansed.

More dangerous than physical germs is the disease of sin. The Scriptures repeatedly picture washing as the means to be cleansed from it. After David's sin with Bathsheba, he declared, "Wash me thoroughly from my iniquity, and cleanse me from my sin. . . . Purge me with hyssop, and I shall be clean: wash me, and I shall be whiter than snow" (Ps. 51:2, 7).

In a salvific sense, this washing comes through Christ's shed blood, as the Apostle John attests, "Jesus Christ, the faithful witness . . . who loved us and washed us from our sins in His own blood" (Rev. 1:5).

Washing is also used as a picture of ongoing sanctification. As Christ sanctifies the Church as His eternal bride, so too are earthly husbands to sanctify their wives through the use of God's precious Word:

> *Husbands, love your wives, even as Christ also loved the church, and gave himself for it; That he might sanctify and cleanse it with the washing of water by the word, That he might present it to himself a glorious church, not having spot, or wrinkle, or any such thing; but that it should be holy and without blemish. (Eph. 5:25-27)*

This "washing of water by the word" (Eph. 5:26) is to be a personal act of love, as a husband cleanses his wife's rough spots to make her more beautiful and radiant.

While the husband's love for his wife is what is in view here, a wife should also be spurred on by love whenever she seeks to address sin in her husband's life.

Looking to the Proverbs 31 woman as an example, a virtuous wife should do her husband "good and not evil all the days of her life" (Prov. 31:12). Though she is to always "reverence her husband" (Eph. 5:33), there are times where respectfully addressing sin in his life is for his good.

God's Word can not only wash the sin of wives; it can also wash the sin of husbands and cleanse them. My friend says, "He who washes his wife in the Word, also gets a bath." Its sanctifying power can transform our marriages, making us more like Christ each day.

To Correct or Not to Correct: A Matter of Love

With this by way of backdrop, what should you do when your spouse sins? Should you correct? Should you go where angels fear to tread? When does an infraction rise to the level where reproof is necessary?

To answer these questions, we must first ensure that love for our spouse is framing our perspective and motivations. This will help us evaluate the situation properly and act as we should.

Love does not harbor petty offences. So if you're about to confront your husband or wife over some minor infraction, stop and change course.

Both Solomon and Peter speak to this: "The discretion of a man makes him slow to anger, and his glory is to overlook a transgression" (Prov. 19:11); "And above all things have fervent love for one another, for 'love will cover a multitude of sins'" (1 Pet. 4:8).

There are times, however, when love requires confrontation. Solomon makes this clear: "Open rebuke is better than love carefully concealed. Faithful are the wounds of a friend" (Prov. 27:5-6).

Moses declared that a needed rebuke is an act of love. And there are times when to neglect that needed rebuke is an act of hatred (Lev. 19:17-18).

The Lord Jesus Himself told His disciples: "if your brother sins against you, go and tell him his fault between you and him alone. If he hears you, you have gained your brother" (Matt. 18:15).

Yet even when love calls for confrontation, it also governs how it should be carried out. Love demands a careful "heart examination" and thoughtful preparation. Your heart and "bedside manner" matter; you're not free to confront your mate in any old way.

A Seven-Point Heart Check

Paul prescribes a seven-point heart check that must be followed when pursuing confrontation:

> *Brethren, if a man is overtaken in any trespass, you who are spiritual restore such a one in a spirit of gentleness, considering yourself lest you also be tempted. Bear one another's burdens, and so fulfill the law of Christ. For if anyone thinks himself*

to be something, when he is nothing, he deceives himself.
(Gal. 6:1-3)

Checkpoint One: Has your spouse been "overtaken in any trespass" (Gal. 6:1)?

A trespass is not an eccentric quirk. It is not a misstep or an accident. It is not an annoying idiosyncrasy. These are not grounds to upbraid your spouse.

A trespass is a fall. It is "a lapse or deviation from truth and uprightness; a sin, misdeed."[1] It may or may not be premeditated. It may be unintentional (there are unintentional sins). The whole armor of God was not in place. Perhaps your mate was particularly vulnerable because of underlying sins.

Make sure you are evaluating your spouse's actions against this standard. And only move forward with correction if they have truly trespassed.

Checkpoint Two: Are you spiritually-minded or earthly-minded (Gal. 6:1)?

Is your mind "filled with the knowledge of His will in all wisdom and spiritual understanding" (Col. 1:9), or is it carnal in nature? You must get to the bottom of this before proceeding.

In the text immediately preceding this seven-pronged test, Paul explains what being spiritually minded looks like:

> *But the fruit of the Spirit is love, joy, peace, longsuffering, kindness, goodness, faithfulness, gentleness, self-control. Against such there is no law. And those who are Christ's have crucified the flesh with its passions and desires. If we live in the Spirit, let us also walk in the Spirit. Let us not become conceited, provoking one another, envying one another. (Gal. 5:22-26)*

---

1 *paraptōma* (G3900 in *Strong's*), definition in *Thayer's Greek Lexicon* (1896).

Being Spirit-driven rather than flesh-driven when you confront someone is crucial, "for to be carnally minded is death, but to be spiritually minded is life and peace" (Rom. 8:6)—so be sure to get this right before you correct your spouse!

Checkpoint Three: Are you pursuing the right objective—to "restore such a one" (Gal. 6:1)?

The word "restore" speaks of putting a dislocated limb back in place. The word is also used of fishermen mending their nets.[2] A process of repair is implied in this metaphor. As you weigh your words, be aware that your speech will always take you in a particular direction, so make sure your words take you to the right destination. When dealing with a spouse "overtaken in any trespass" (Gal. 6:1), drive toward restoration, and don't say anything that would divert you from this end. Do not allow emotions to cloud your vision. Don't let offenses get in the way of this primary objective.

Checkpoint Four: Are you operating in a "spirit of gentleness" (Gal. 6:1)?

Gentleness is a fruit of the Spirit (Gal. 5:23) that is required of Christians when they bring correction:

> *And a servant of the Lord must not quarrel but be gentle to all, able to teach, patient, in humility correcting those who are in opposition, if God perhaps will grant them repentance, so that they may know the truth, and that they may come to their senses and escape the snare of the devil, having been taken captive by him to do his will. (2 Tim. 2:24-26)*

---

2 On putting back a dislocated limb, see: John MacArthur, *Galatians: The MacArthur New Testament Commentary* (Chicago: Moody Publishers, 1987), p. 179. On mending nets, see: William Hendriksen, *Galatians and Ephesians: New Testament Commentary by William Hendriksen* (Grand Rapids, Baker Book House, 1979), p. 232.

Gentleness is powerful. It usually de-escalates tension. It often brings the other party to their senses. "A soft answer turns away wrath" (Prov. 15:1). Gentleness acts like a shock absorber. It smooths the bumps. Our appeals should be cushioned with gentleness and respect (1 Pet. 3:15). We should manifest the way of our Lord Jesus who is "gentle and lowly in heart" (Matt. 11:29-30).

Regardless of the outcome, the Bible tells us that gentleness is like clothing. It is our outward appearance. Christians ought to be clothed with gentleness (Col. 3:12).

If you are tempted to kick your spouse while they're down, you are not ready to restore. Take a deep breath. Ask the Lord to give you a calm and tender spirit. As you enter into discussion with them, take time to prepare yourself for mercy. Be clothed with gentleness.

Checkpoint Five: Are you recognizing your own shortcomings? (Gal. 6:1)

Before confronting your mate who is "overtaken in any trespass," Paul says to "[consider] yourself lest you also be tempted" (Gal. 6:1). This calls for self-awareness.

Are you acknowledging that you too are a sinner? Are you searching your own heart for the same sin? Looking at yourself means to make careful observation of what's lurking inside. If you have elements of the same sin present within you, you must deal with it before confronting your spouse's sin, as Jesus taught:

> *And why do you look at the speck in your brother's eye, but do not consider the plank in your own eye? Or how can you say to your brother, "Let me remove the speck from your eye"; and look, a plank is in your own eye? Hypocrite! First remove the plank from your own eye, and then you will see clearly to remove the speck from your brother's eye. (Matt. 7:3-5)*

Checkpoint Six: Are you prepared to keep bearing a burden? (Gal. 6:2)

Paul calls us to "Bear one another's burdens, and so fulfill the law of Christ" (Gal. 6:2). Are you willing to bear the weight of your husband or wife? How long are you willing to bear it? We often want quick results. We want to get everything resolved *now*! When we are in a difficult conversation that does not seem to be producing good results, patience often means that we "extend help to the brother so that he may overcome his spiritual weakness."[3] This requires patience.

Our Lord Jesus Christ has been very patient with us. How patient has He been with you? Did He require perfection of you immediately? Christ modeled such loving sacrifice on the cross as He "[bore] our griefs and carried our sorrows" (Isa. 53:4). His shouldering of man's sin is the only path to ultimate forgiveness and salvation. Before you pursue confrontation, make sure you are ready to patiently bear the weight of disappointment and to keep bearing it until the Lord chooses to relieve the burden.

Checkpoint Seven: Are you self-effacing or condescending? (Gal. 6:3)

Paul punctuates his seven-pronged heart check on confrontation with this hefty punch: "if anyone thinks himself to be something, when he is nothing, he deceives himself" (Gal. 6:3).

So here's the question: Do you think you are better and wiser than your mate who's been "overtaken in any trespass" (Gal. 6:1)? Then utterly banish this thought! A disdainfully superior attitude has no place when you confront a fallen husband or wife. If this is your inner disposition, you need to humble yourself before acting.

A spirit of superiority is a reconciliation killer. If you do not conquer this destructive sin, it will linger in your marriage and harm your spouse.

---

3   Hendriksen, pp. 232-233.

Conclusion

"Reproofs of instruction are the way of life" (Prov. 6:23). That's the clear teaching of Scripture.

God's Word is the basis for this "reproof" (2 Tim. 3:16). With it we are washed and sanctified and made more like Christ (Eph. 5:26-27).

This is a process we should welcome in our married life.

The truth is, we often need reproof because it is hard to break bad patterns. Worse still, we are often blind to them. We thus need help.

And our spouse—our one-flesh partner who sees us up close on our good and bad days—is often uniquely equipped to recognize our sins and give God's Word as a healing corrective.

Such purging will not only purify our lives (Eph. 5:26-27), but it will fortify us as well, for "he who has clean hands shall be stronger and stronger" (Job 17:9).

"The ear that hears the rebukes of life will abide among the wise" (Prov. 15:31).

As you are learning to paint well, remember that you are painting a picture of mutual sanctification by the washing of water by the Word, an image of progressive purity.

As a loving spouse, paint pictures of willingness to give and receive reproof, as needed, so that your marriage will be marked by greater purity, strength, and wisdom.

Questions

1. Are you open to correction?

2. Are you correcting one another in the spirit that God describes in Galatians 6?

CHAPTER 9

You Don't Need to Fix Everything

*And above all things have fervent love for one another, for
'love will cover a multitude of sins.' (1 Pet. 4:8)*

In the biblical picture of marriage you find imperfections,
patiently endured and covered over.

When a couple wants to fix their marriage, they tend to focus
on the problems. Their sins are making life hard. They are always
asking, "How can I fix this?" They identify the sins. They name
them one by one. They understand the destructive power that sin
can cause in their marriage, so they are set on rooting it out. They
get on an improvement path.

Yet sometimes they go on the warpath against one another.
They point fingers. They repeatedly name sins. In their efforts to
"fix" troubled spots they overreach and vaporize "love, joy, peace,
patience [and] kindness . . ." (Gal. 5:22, ESV).

They are, in effect, spraying Roundup all over the place.

In farming we spray the "cides"—insecticides, pesticides, and
herbicides. Couples often use the "cides." They are on a mission
to kill the harmful pests in their marriages. They get everything
out on the table. They make lists. They track the infractions. They
share their disappointments. They're constantly analyzing their
partner's sin and confronting them about it.

Their incessant question is, "How are we doing?" They are
obsessed with having everything sorted out. If it's not going well,
they keep spraying the "cides" on one another and fogging up the
room.

In nit-picking every blemish, they do more harm than good.

Make no mistake—it is right and appropriate to deal with sins and to have hard conversations to work through them (Prov. 27:5-6). Sin is the greatest enemy of our marriages. That's why it is good for us to identify its painful consequences (Gal. 6:7-9). Our life as Christians must be a life of mortifying sin (Col. 3:5-8), turning from evil (1 Pet. 3:11), and hating it (Ps. 97:10), for we are to "Abhor what is evil [and] cling to what is good" (Rom. 12:9).

Yet you can't make a good marriage by chronic analysis and harping. At some point you need to quit dissecting and confronting and remember that "love will cover a multitude of sins" (1 Pet. 4:8). That's what love does. Rather than engage in vain repetitions, "Love suffers long and is kind" (1 Cor. 13:4). In dealing with our spouse, we are to walk "with all lowliness and gentleness, with longsuffering, bearing with one another in love" (Eph. 4:2).

How to Cover Sin: Choke It Out with God's Word

Let me illustrate what it looks like to cover over sin in a healthy way.

When you are raising cattle, you first must raise grass. It takes time to cultivate pastures so that they are productive. It involves seeding, cultivating, fertilizing, and watering. It requires sun and heat. The grass needs all of these elements to thrive.

My wife and I have dealt with this personally. We had lots of weeds in one of our pastures, which made it hard to provide adequate grass for the cows. Our reaction was to turn to weed killer, but we didn't know what kind of herbicide to use. So we talked to some people who sprayed. And we spoke to some experienced farmers about how to turn it around. In response they simply said:

You just need to choke out the weeds by planting grass. Don't ruin your pasture with defoliants. If you do a good job planting seeds and taking care of them, the grass will consume the nutrients, and the weeds won't have a chance.

So, instead of resorting to weed killer, we decided to spend our money on seed instead. What do you know? After we planted, watered, and fertilized, we had the best grass ever with hardly any weeds!

Marriage is like growing grass to choke out the weeds. The soil of your marriage needs water, sun, and nutrients. In a marriage, the Word of God cultivates. It breaks up the fallow ground of our hearts and plants good seeds (Heb. 4:12; Hos. 10:12; Luke 8:11). The filling of the Holy Spirit provides water and nutrients, nurturing us with life-giving truth (John 6:63; 16:13; 2 Cor. 3:5-6).

This is the most effective way to get rid of the weeds in your marriage. You choke them out by focusing on the Lord and His ways. When you are "filled up with all the fullness of God" (Eph. 3:19), the weeds wither and die. They can't survive this truth-rich atmosphere, as God's Word takes root and displaces them.

He Who Began a Good Work Will Complete It

Christ will sanctify you and your mate over the long haul. Of this you can be sure. If you know the Lord, you can be "confident of this very thing, that He who has begun a good work in you will complete *it* until the day of Jesus Christ" (Phil. 1:6). Once your earthly walk is done, He will take you to your heavenly home, and you will sin no more.

If you understand this reality, you can accept your spouse for your short earthly stay on this earth together. Remember that love "bears all things" (1 Cor. 13:7). It gives us the ability to walk patiently with others, "The discretion of a man makes him slow to anger, And his glory is to overlook a transgression" (Prov. 19:11).

Charles Spurgeon put it this way: "Where love is thin, there faults are always thick. Wherever there is true love in the heart, we make many . . . allowances for the weaknesses and infirmities of our friends."[1]

The lesson is clear—don't be obsessed with your spouse's shortcomings!

Love Your Spouse in Their Weakness

Just the other day, I was observing my wife in a moment of one of her weaknesses. I smiled. It was not a serious sin. It's just that one of the manifestations of the Fall showed itself in her. "It's kind of cute," I thought.

I'm not saying that sin is cute. I'm saying that I know God is going to keep working with her. What I saw made me love her more, not less. It also made me love the Lord more for His atoning sacrifice, His patience, His kindness, and His love toward her—a love He shows me, as well, in all of my frailties as a husband.

My bride's virtues far outweigh her sins. I know that God will ultimately heal her. She has already been forgiven—past, present, and future. God will put her shortcomings behind her in His own good time. In the meantime, I'm at peace; I don't need to fix everything in my wife. This is "the time to embrace" (Eccl. 3:5).

---

1   C.H. Spurgeon, "Luminous Words," A Sermon Delivered on Lord's Day Evening, December 28, 1884, at The Metropolitan Tabernacle, Newington.

Conclusion

As you are getting the picture right, remember that lovingly covering your spouse's blemishes should be part of the portrait. So paint pictures of tender mercies!

Like growing grass, it takes time to choke out the weeds. We choke them out by sowing seeds, adding water, and shining the sun. Like Adam and Eve, we are gardeners.

So, smile along the way! You don't need to fix everything in your marriage. You can't fix everything in your marriage. But you can choke out the weeds by degrees with the good things, enlivened through God's Spirit, in His Word (John 16:13).

Do not be deceived, God is not mocked; for whatever a man sows, that he will also reap. For he who sows to his flesh will of the flesh reap corruption, but he who sows to the Spirit will of the Spirit reap everlasting life. And let us not grow weary while doing good, for in due season we shall reap if we do not lose heart. (Gal. 6:7-9)

Questions

1. Are you chronically obsessed with the imperfections of your marriage, and what areas of imperfection are best to be covered over?

2. Explain: How does the work of the Holy Spirit help you to bear the weaknesses of your spouse?

CHAPTER 10

Don't Let Sexual Intimacy Die in Your Marriage

Let the husband render to his wife the affection due her, and likewise also the wife to her husband. . . . Do not deprive one another (1 Cor. 7:3,5)

In the biblical portrait of marriage, you find enduring sexual intimacy. The oneness of the marriage bed is a poignant picture of Christ's love for His church. As shocking as it might seem, the sexual union is to reflect Christ's intimacy with His bride. Married couples become living pictures of it, as they are naked and not ashamed.

When a husband and wife come together sexually, it is very important that they think rightly about what this coupling means. Physical oneness is not simply the union of bodies. The Bible makes it clear that the closeness of the sexual union is an earthly picture of the closeness of the union believers have with Christ:

'For this reason a man shall leave his father and mother and be joined to his wife, and the two shall become one flesh.' This is a great mystery, but I speak concerning Christ and the church. (Eph. 5:31-32)

What is this one-flesh union supposed to look like? It is to represent the joy, the unity, the covenant, the comfort, the tenderness, the security, the patience, the lack of shame, and the exclusivity we have in Christ as His bride. When you make love as husband and wife, you are painting an ornate and graphic picture.

Intimacy is inherent and essential to marriage. God desires for you to be close—very close—skin to skin. History and the Bible open with this theme, as God crowned creation week by bringing Adam and Eve together to "know" one another as "one flesh" (Gen. 2:24; 4:1).

This oneness in marriage is an expression of God's closeness and ever-increasing conformity and oneness with His people. God is one and He is one with His children. Jonathan Edward states:

> *He sees the ever-increasing union between himself and his creatures all at once. He sees their conformity to his image as it looks from the eternal point of view, which must appear to him as a perfect nearness, conformity, unity, and oneness.*[1]

Sex in Marriage: Three Things God Forbids

Yet, while sexual union within marriage is wonderfully pleasurable and speaks of the wonder of Christ and His church, the Devil is always at the door to destroy and pervert it. Thankfully, we're not left to flounder, as God has given precepts and principles that protect, guide, and ensure that sexual intimacy remains sacred. He created it as good, but He condemns three things regarding sex in marriage that are evil.

First, God condemns adultery. This includes sex outside of marriage (Ex. 20:14) as well as adultery of the heart (Matt. 5:28). Not only is sleeping with someone other than your spouse forbidden, but so too is lusting after any person (real or imagined).

Second, He condemns immoral affections and actions within marriage. This includes the use of pornography (voyeurism) and domination between married couples, along with any other selfish and impure thoughts or acts that are contrary to the explicit commands of God (Matt. 5:28; Eph. 5:3; Heb. 13:4).

---

1   Edwards, p. 77.

Third, He condemns sexual starvation within marriage. This involves depriving one another of sexual intimacy (1 Cor. 7:3-5).

All three of these vices, if left unchecked, will damage your marriage. They all paint an ugly picture.

A Wife's Challenge: Afraid to Touch

Most couples experience differences in desire, frequency, location, timing, and methods of sexual intimacy. When it's bedtime, it is common for a wife to be afraid to touch her husband, because she knows that if she merely touches him in a particular way, sex is going to happen. And it will happen pretty quickly. And she doesn't feel like she's ready. So she's hesitant to touch her spouse. She knows his biology and his psychology.

So you have this conundrum. A wife may want to snuggle up with her husband, but she is afraid to do so because of his predictable response. And it is a real problem because it is good for husbands and wives to snuggle up. It is a comfort to both parties. It is a blessing. It is protective.

Yet you can find wives who don't touch their husbands because they're afraid he will immediately turn to sex.

A Husband's Challenge: An Uncomfortable Conversation

On the flip side, husbands often get frustrated with their wife's tepid response in the bedroom.

It is legendary that men end up wanting to have an uncomfortable conversation. The sexual activity in their marriage is less than the husband desires. He tolerates it for a while, but then he feels he needs to say something. He wants to say it, but he is afraid to bring it up. He doesn't want to discourage his wife. He doesn't want her to think that he is disappointed in her. He doesn't want to force her to do anything.

So, at some point, that husband will venture into a conversation. It might go something like this, "I wish you desired me more. Why don't you? You never initiate. It seems like you are spurning me when I want to make love."

A Framework to Sort through Differences

The Apostle Paul gives a clear framework for sorting through these differences:

> *Let the husband render to his wife the affection due her, and likewise also the wife to her husband. The wife does not have authority over her own body, but the husband does. And likewise the husband does not have authority over his own body, but the wife does. Do not deprive one another except with consent for a time, that you may give yourselves to fasting and prayer; and come together again so that Satan does not tempt you because of your lack of self-control. (1 Cor. 7:3-5)*

We learn three lessons here.

Lesson One: Render Due Affection

First, sexual intimacy is to be freely rendered between husbands and wives as affection that is due (1 Cor. 7:3).

The word "render" means to "discharge what is due," so sex within marriage is a holy obligation.[2] It is an integral duty, not a severable option that can be set aside.

Even as sex is to be freely given, the word "affection" speaks of the heart that should envelop both parties in this sacred act.

Affection means, "friendly disposition, well disposed; attached; goodwill."[3] Sex should thus be an act of friendly

---

2 *apodidōmi* (G551) in Strongs: definition of "render" from J. H. Thayer, Thayer's Greek Definitions (1896).

3 As defined in: G. Kittel, G. W. Bromiley, & G. Friedrich (Eds.), *Theological Dictionary of the New Testament* (electronic ed., Vol. 4, pp. 971–972). Eerdmans, 1964.

goodwill toward one's spouse, not a selfish pursuit. A husband and wife should pay attention to what communicates affection to their partner and supply it. They should focus on giving, not taking. They should seek to increase their spouse's pleasure, first and foremost, not their own. They should love their spouse "as their own bodies" (Eph. 5:28).

Couples need to think on three levels simultaneously: first, affection ("how beautiful . . . you are," Song of Sol. 7:6-9, ESV); second, satisfaction ("let her breasts satisfy you," Prov. 5:15-19); and, third, obligation (1 Cor. 7:3-5).

Though it is to be pursued in the most caring way, sex within marriage is "affection due" (1 Cor. 7:3). To quote John MacArthur, it "is not an option or an extra."[4]

Lesson Two: Mutual Authority—Our Bodies Are Not Our Own

Second, husbands and wives share mutual authority over their spouse's body where sexual intimacy is concerned.

Paul writes, "The wife does not have authority over her own body, but the husband does. And likewise the husband does not have authority over his own body, but the wife does" (1 Cor. 7:4).

God teaches us that when we marry, our bodies are not our own. We surrender them to our spouses. We are thus to defer to our partner's wishes in the bedroom in order to please them.

This is real authority. Each one has rights over the other. This triggers serving one another. The command facilitates loving service—both ways.

Lesson Three: Do Not Deprive One Another

So what if one spouse chronically insists on abstinence, while the other desires more frequent sexual intimacy? How can "mutual submission" be logically resolved?

---

4   On 1 Corinthians 7:3-5: John MacArthur, *1 Corinthians: The MacArthur New Testament Commentary* (Chicago: Moody Publishers, 1984), p. 157.

Paul has already established that sexual intimacy is to be freely rendered between husbands and wives as affection that is due (1 Cor. 7:3).

But he then doubles down with another explicit command. His third point is this—married couples are not to deprive each other of physical oneness except for a short, mutually agreed-upon season:

> *Do not deprive one another except with consent for a time, that you may give yourselves to fasting and prayer; and come together again so that Satan does not tempt you because of your lack of self-control. (1 Cor. 7:5)*

We are commanded not to "deprive," which is to cause someone not to possess something. Rather, we are to do what the other person wants to do within the lawful boundaries of holy union. You are not your own in a marriage. What your spouse wants to do matters.

This does not mean that one spouse can force the other to perform lewd acts or what goes against nature. Love is not like that. True love always conforms to God's beautiful order of how He created "male and female" (Gen. 1:27), and neither partner is free to insist on anything that goes against it. "Affection due" is that which follows God's design.

Though loving deference is to be shown to one's partner (which sometimes means no sex), sexual union is to be the prevailing, regular pattern between couples. Special times of "fasting and prayer" are cause for temporary abstinence. As are physical challenges by either partner, such as a woman's period (Lev. 18:19). But these are to be the exceptions, not the norm. The norm should be regular sexual intimacy. Relations should be promptly resumed after a consensual break, and this should be the goal from the outset.

Paul heightens the point by warning how Satan will use extended sexual abstinence between husbands and wives as bait to tempt them with illicit sexual thoughts or actions outside marriage (1 Cor. 7:5). Matthew Henry notes, "If they abstain from lawful enjoyments, they may be ensnared into unlawful ones."[5] To stave off this temptation, couples should come together again.

The mutual authority Paul cites (1 Cor. 7:4) should not lead to an irreconcilable stand-off, for He tips the scales in favor of regular sex with these two commands: "render . . . the affection due" and "do not deprive one another" (1 Cor. 7:3, 5). While abstaining out of a spirit of love is sometimes in order, these scriptural mandates should shape the overall pattern of the marriage bed.

A sex-starved marriage is not only against God's design; it is rebellion against His explicit commands. As a general rule, spouses are to relinquish themselves in mutual affection when the other party shows desire.

Five Barriers to Intimacy

Many barriers can hamper the sexual relationship. In order to troubleshoot these barriers, they need to be clearly identified and addressed.

Physical Challenges

First, your sexual activity may be hampered by physical challenges such as hormonal imbalances, infections, or inadequate lubrication. Then there are the obvious changes to the body that come with age.

Couples grappling with such conditions that prevent sexual intimacy will need to agree on thoughtful "workarounds." In other words, they need to find ways to bring pleasure to one another if intercourse is too painful or simply not possible.

---

5   On 1 Cor. 7:1-9: Matthew Henry, *Commentary on the Whole Bible* (1811).

Past Sexual Abuse

Second, sexual abuse in your past may make you wary of intercourse. When your spouse initiates intimacy, heartbreaking memories flood in. Recollections of rape or incest or other forms of rejecting the beauty of God's design still haunt you. You were made to think that sex was filthy. It may even be terrifying to you. When you are with your spouse, these past ugly scenes engulf your thoughts, and you hate it.

If this is your plight, then turn to God who is more than able to heal you:

> *He has sent Me to heal the brokenhearted To proclaim liberty to the captives, And the opening of the prison to those who are bound, . . . To comfort all who mourn, To console those who mourn in Zion, To give them beauty for ashes, The oil of joy for mourning, The garment of praise for the spirit of heaviness; That they may be called trees of righteousness, The planting of the LORD, that He may be glorified. (Isa. 61:1-3)*

The Belief that Sex Is Dirty

Third, your hesitance for intimacy may be influenced by the wrong view that sex within marriage is dirty and sinful.

The Medieval Roman Catholic Church propounded this falsehood and forbade sex on holy days.[6] Celibacy was elevated above marriage because sex was viewed as carnal and beneath the behavior of a faithful saint.

Yet the witness of Scripture condemns this notion: "Marriage is honorable among all, and the bed undefiled" (Heb. 13:4).

If this false view of sex has infected your thinking, then dispense with it.

---

6   Joe Boot, "Sex and the History of Christianity," *Ezra Institute* (Blog), April 1, 2013. Accessed July 14, 2023, https://www.ezrainstitute.com/resource-library/articles/sex-and-the-history-of-christianity/.

The Poison of Pornography

Fourth, your disinterest in physical oneness with your spouse may be driven by the poison of pornography.

Learning from porn will make you a failure at love. It is like going to a weird business school where they teach you how to fail in business.

Pornography is self-worship. It drives you to objectify another person as merely a "pretty" tool to satiate your selfish lusts. In pornography, you are a taker. You use another person for your own greedy pleasure. Yet real relationships don't thrive in the cesspool of such idolatry. This is why people poisoned by pornography often experience sexual dysfunction in marriage. They get bored with their real-life spouse who fails to live up to their raunchy fantasies.

On the other hand, if your spouse is caught up in pornography, you will likely feel cheapened and may resist sex for that reason.

The sin of porn calls for drastic action. It is a false teacher that must be banished. In order to fulfill the picture of heavenly exaltation, pureness and fidelity, driven by sacrificial love, must take its place. We are sons and daughters of the King. This means that we must keep the picture right. We must be manifesting Christ's love for His church, and the church's respect for her husband (Eph. 5:22-33). The matter is non-negotiable.

There should be no hint of sexual immorality in your marriage (Eph. 5:3; Heb. 13:4; 1 Cor. 6:9; 1 Cor. 6:18; 1 Thess. 4:3-5). And, if there is, you must deal with it immediately, for it will defile both you and your spouse. Do not think on or otherwise use pornography in your marriage bed. Instead, "let her breasts satisfy you"; "be enraptured by her love" (Prov. 5:19); and embrace your nakedness without shame (Gen. 2:25).

Expect that the Devil will attack you on these grounds, for he "walks about like a roaring lion, seeking whom he may devour" (1 Pet. 5:8). In today's world of smart phones and laptops, porn is only a click away. Out of love for God and your spouse, resolve to "make no provision for the flesh, to fulfill its lusts" (Rom. 13:14).

The Guilt of Past Sins

Fifth, you or your spouse may be gun-shy about sex because of guilt you're carrying from past sinful behavior. Perhaps you were sexually promiscuous before marriage or used to have a bad porn problem. Or maybe you have shame for having heartless or even perverted sex with your spouse earlier in your married life. Perhaps, conversely, your partner has been guilty of one or more of these ugly sins.

True repentance and forgiveness are the only way out of this mess: "If we confess our sins, he is faithful and just to forgive us our sins and to cleanse us from all unrighteousness" (1 John 1:9).

Just as God will forgive you if you come to Him in genuine contrition, so you must be willing to forgive one another:

> *Let all bitterness, wrath, anger, clamor, and evil speaking be put away from you, with all malice. And be kind to one another, tenderhearted, forgiving one another, just as God in Christ forgave you. (Eph. 4:31-32)*

Most married couples are in a recovery program from selfish sin patterns that the world taught them about sex. The good news is that if you come to God in humble repentance, He can restore what has been lost (Isa. 66:2; Joel 2:25-26). And, by His grace, you can pursue a wholesome sex life bathed in purity, moving ahead.

Sexual Desire in Wives: A Theory

Why is it that, in general, the wife has a harder time with sexual intimacy than the husband does? I know this is not universal. But from my experience in counseling with couples and reading studies on the matter, the majority of wives seem to experience less desire compared to their husbands.

This often presents a challenge to the husband. He finds himself in a position where he realizes his wife does not have the same desires for him as he does for her. She is not as responsive as he wishes. She does not initiate. She does not seem interested.

Why is this?

I have a theory. It comes from the fact that the wife distinctively represents the church. The Lord compares the wife to the church. She is a glorious church loved by Christ, her husband (Eph. 5:25-27). But Christians (the church) often experience an uneven love for Christ in return. We go up and down. We are not consistent in our passion and service for God. We go through seasons when we hunger for the Lord. We go through seasons when our desire diminishes.

Perhaps the wife represents this in her sexual desire.

A woman's menstrual cycle might be pointing to the same thing in the way that her period causes mood swings. She may feel depressed, hopeless, and even become fitful. Believers go through these same kinds of cycles in their relationship with the Lord. Perhaps this is a picture of what happens to the church. She experiences ups and downs, but the husband maintains his devotion to her through it all.

A wife struggling with sexual desire may be a picture of the church and how she struggles with desire for prayer and the Word of God and service. Yet even in her weakness, she has a devoted husband. Her groom keeps pursuing her. He seeks her, draws her near, and shows His undying love for her.

A wife's cycles teach a husband to love his wife through all her ups and downs. In God's sanctifying grace, He draws a husband into more love through his wife's weakness. His love is tested by her ups and downs. But the testing is good. Through the testing the husband learns what love really is.

Find the Root Problem and Deal with It

God is not in favor of letting sex die in your marriage. If you have lost the desire for physical oneness with your mate, you must know that it is only a symptom.

Perhaps you have done something or thought something that has allowed distance. Can you identify the source of that distance?

The way to close the divide is to understand why you have little desire and learn how to fan it to flame. And if it is sinful thoughts that are causing the distance, then the solution is to repent by turning away from them.

Remember to Reflect Christ's Love for His Church

Someone once said that the mind is the primary sexual organ. This is true. Your thinking always governs your acting. You thus need to remember that you are to reflect Christ's love for His church when you make love. You should be thinking of your one-flesh bond with your spouse as holy and beautiful and selfless in the way Christ's bond with His bride is.

When you come to the marriage bed, turn your mind to the compassion of Christ, the sacrificial giving of Christ, the loving service of Christ, and pleasure that is in Christ which points to the sexual union. All of this is a picture of Christ and His church.

Commenting on this rich parallel, Charles Spurgeon declared:

> *Our marriage union with husband or wife cannot be more clear, more sure, more matter of fact, than our oneness with Christ and our enjoyment of that oneness. Joy! joy! joy! He whom we love is ours!*[7]

---

7   Charles H. Spurgeon, Sermon No. 1634B, "Loved and Loving: Among the Apple Trees," Metropolitan Tabernacle Pulpit 1, Volume 27.

Do you view your spouse with such deep love and joy? If not, let the reality of Christ's love for His church cleanse your heart and mind and reframe your approach to intimacy with your mate.

Remember Your Wedding Vows

When you face moments or days or weeks when you simply do not feel like being one with your spouse, you must remember your Bible and your wedding vows. The vows are all tied to Scripture. It is easy to subtly break these solemn pledges by refusing to engage in sexual intimacy. You must examine your heart, for where sex-starved marriages exist, sinful disobedience exists.

Refusing to let sex die in your marriage is one way that you declare—over and over again—that you are married, that you are not your own, and that you are loving your spouse the way Christ loves His church.

As you are learning to paint pictures of Christ's love, remember that you are painting a graphically close, humbly tender, and shockingly ecstatic picture of Christ and His church.

Christ's love for His bride is constant and everlasting (Jer. 31:3), and, in like manner, our desire for our spouse should never be quenched:

> *Let your fountain be blessed, And rejoice with the wife of your youth. As a loving deer and a graceful doe, Let her breasts satisfy you at all times; And always be enraptured with her love. (Prov. 5:18-19)*

Questions

1. Is there any identifiable barrier from your sin or past experience that is keeping you apart sexually?

2. How can you make sexual intimacy to be more like giving and submission and less like taking and personal gratification?

CHAPTER 11

—————————➤

How to Quell Contempt

*Let nothing be done through selfish ambition or conceit, but
in lowliness of mind let each esteem others better than himself.
Let each of you look out not only for his own interests, but also
for the interests of others. Let this mind be in you which was
also in Christ Jesus. (Phil. 2:3-5)*

In the biblical picture of marriage you find compassions, new
every morning. You are painting pictures of affection. The
opposite of affection is contempt.

Sadly, marriages are often like volcanoes of contempt. While
contempt is a secret sin, it comes out in pictures. Evil sins such
as anger, bitterness, and pride grow through stages under the
surface until they finally erupt.

Volcanos are predictable in this sense. First there are
earthquake swarms. Then gas emissions. Then steam and lava.
Then ash starts venting. Pressure builds deep down. Magma
and gas become so hot (sometimes exceeding 2,000 degrees
Fahrenheit) that they melt. They reach a boiling point. Gas rises
to the surface. Then destruction follows.

Some volcanoes blow up like Mt. St. Helens and are deadly.
Others move slowly and cause lava to flow above ground, slowly
devouring anything in its path. The magma and the gas finally
rupture for all to see.

Relationships can be like that.

With volcanoes, eruptions are often triggered by earthquakes
that occur miles beneath the earth's surface. That's where

marriage problems begin—out of sight in the deepest recesses of the heart. They start with secret sins, hidden meditations, and covered-up attitudes. If left unchecked, these destructive vices boil and then blow.

Contempt: Marriage's Biggest Destroyer

Contempt is one such devastating sin. Most people get married with little or no contempt for one another. During the honeymoon stage, infatuation reigns. But once this wears off, opportunities for contempt are very real. Little things that never bothered couples before, now annoy them. The pressure builds.

Dr. John Gottman, one of the world's foremost marriage researchers, has spent forty years studying marriages and their dissolution. After decades of interviewing couples, he concluded that the number one cause of divorce is contempt.[1] I am not a statistician, but from my experience with marriage counseling, it makes enormous sense.

The Gottman Institute gives these common outbursts of contempt:

> *Treating others with disrespect and mocking them with sarcasm and condescension are forms of contempt. So are hostile humor, name-calling, mimicking, and body language such as eye-rolling and sneering.[2]*

And what's at the heart of this festering volcano?

---

1   Marissa Gold, "This Is the Number One Predictor of Divorce—and How to Fix It," *Woman's Day*, February 19, 2016. Accessed August 4, 2023, https://www.womansday.com/relationships/dating-marriage/a53790/contempt-and-divorce/
2   Ellie Lisitsa, "The Four Horsemen: Contempt," The Gottman Institute (Blog). Accessed August 4, 2022, https://www.gottman.com/blog/the-four-horsemen-contempt/?rq=contempt.

*In whatever form [it erupts], contempt is poisonous to a
relationship because it conveys disgust and superiority. . . .
Contempt, simply put, says, "I'm better than you. And you are
lesser than me."³*

Contempt Defined and Condemned

The Oxford English Dictionary defines contempt as, "The action
of contemning or despising; the holding or treating [someone or
something] as of little account, . . . the mental attitude in which
a thing is so considered."⁴

Where relationships are concerned, contempt comes about
when you view someone else as inferior to yourself because of
some real or perceived weakness. You haughtily look down your
nose at them because they don't "measure up." For one reason or
another, you consider yourself better than them.

The Scriptures squarely condemn this posture:

*Let nothing be done through selfish ambition or conceit, but
in lowliness of mind let each esteem others better than himself.
Let each of you look out not only for his own interests, but also
for the interests of others. Let this mind be in you which was
also in Christ Jesus. (Phil. 2:3-5)*

How Contempt Builds and Erupts

When we view ourselves too highly and fail to put others
first, the smallest shortcomings in our mate can perturb and
even offend us. And harboring such offenses is often the soil
of contempt. When a spouse becomes offended, contempt can
start to grow.

It starts with shrugging the shoulders. Then the eyes roll.
Complaints begin. The pressure builds. Disrespect is entertained.

---

3   *Ibid.*
4   *Oxford English Dictionary*, "contempt (n.)," Second Edition (1989).

Disrespect turns to scorn. And scorn eventually erupts in full-blown contempt.

Like destructive lava, contempt breaks through the surface with outbursts of contention and ridicule. Its harsh disdain can manifest itself in abject disregard and neglect for one's spouse—and even lead to assault. If left unimpeded, these works of the flesh will, in time, cause alienation between a husband and wife. And such alienation, fomented by the hellish lava of contempt, often brings on divorce.

How to Relieve Pressure and Cure Contempt

How do you keep the volcano from blowing and destroying everyone in the lava stream?

To relieve the pressure in our marriages and cure contempt, we must humbly put on the mind of Christ and follow His example (Phil. 2:5).

Here are four ways to accomplish this.

Show Compassion for Our Spouse's Weaknesses

The first way to cure contempt in our marriages is to emulate Christ by showing compassion toward our spouse's weaknesses.

While every one of us "have sinned and fall short of the glory of God" (Rom. 3:23), Christ is without sin and perfect (2 Cor. 5:21; 1 Pet. 2:22; 1 John 3:5). Yet we learn from the Scriptures that He "sympathize[s] with our weaknesses" (Heb. 4:15). Over and over again throughout His earthly ministry, we find that He was "moved with compassion" as He beheld those weaker than Himself (Matt. 14:14; Mark 1:41; Mark 6:34). Rather than scorning us when we don't measure up, we learn that He is "ready to pardon, gracious and merciful, slow to anger, [and] abundant in kindness" (Neh. 9:17).

Looking to the Psalms, we see a striking example of how we, as fallen creatures, are to imitate God in this respect. Our Lord, as well as the man who fears this same Lord, are said to be "gracious and full of compassion" (Ps. 145:8; 112:4). The exact same phrase is used of both. We are to be "gracious and full of compassion," as God is.

We learn elsewhere in the Psalms that God pities us, for "He knows our frame; He remembers that we are dust" (Ps. 103:14).

This truth should grip us as we think of ourselves and our spouse. We all have hands and feet of clay. Apart from God's grace, our "flesh is weak" (Matt. 26:41). So rather than let contempt take hold when we observe our mate's weaknesses, we should respond with heartfelt compassion instead.

Bear the Infirmities of the Weak

Contempt for our spouse's shortcomings should have no place in our marriage, for "We . . . that are strong ought to bear the infirmities of the weak" (Rom. 15:1, KJV). This is the second cure for contempt.

Husbands are explicitly called out on this by the Apostle Peter: "Husbands, likewise, dwell with them with understanding, giving honor to the wife, as to the weaker vessel, and as being heirs together of the grace of life" (1 Pet. 3:7).

Elaborating on this text, John Gill declared that wives are "not [to] be treated with neglect and contempt, or with inhumanity and severity" as the weaker vessel, but "gently and tenderly . . . so a man should bear with, and accommodate himself to the infirmities of his wife."[5]

Whether we're a husband or wife, we should "Bear one another's burdens, and so fulfill the law of Christ" (Gal. 6:2). We are to "sympathize" with our spouse's weaknesses (Heb. 4:14) and willingly shoulder them, as Christ has done for us (Isa. 53:4).

---

5   Commentary on 1 Pet. 3:7: John Gill, *An Exposition of the New Testament, Vol. III* (London: Mathews and Leigh, 1809), p. 557.

Forgive as We Have Been Forgiven

The third way to cure contempt in our marriages is to forgive our husband or wife as Christ has forgiven us.

When we harbor unforgiveness in our heart toward our spouse for small or even big infractions, the lava of contempt will grow. It will increase and overtake our whole being (Gal. 5:9). And as it gains steam it will spill out through harsh words and gestures.

For the redeemed Christian, such a posture is indefensible. Though the wrongs committed against us by our mate can be substantial at times, they are small in comparison to the wrongs we have committed against Almighty God.

"The Parable of the Unforgiving Servant" drives home this point (Matt. 18:21-35). Though the servant in this parable owed a staggering debt of 10,000 talents, the king mercifully forgave him. Yet showing no regard for this kindness, this ungrateful man refused to forgive a fellow servant a mere hundred pence that was owed to him.

To put these debts in perspective, the yearly gold that King Solomon received while ruling Israel was 666 talents (1 Kings 10:14). Ten thousand talents is fifteen times this amount, so it would take Solomon a decade and a half to receive this much gold in revenue as his nation's sovereign. In contrast to this, a hundred pence represented four months' pay for a common laborer during New Testament times.[6]

Four months' pay for a commoner's work is no small sum, but it is a trifle compared to what the richest king in Israel's history received over fifteen years.

In considering one's marriage, the takeaway should be clear: we who have been forgiven much by Christ should freely forgive our spouse whose sins are far less.

---

6 John MacArthur, *Matthew 16-23: The MacArthur New Testament Commentary* (Chicago: Moody Publishers, 1988), pp. 151-152.

Rather than respond to our mate's sins with contempt, we should follow Christ's example:

Let all bitterness, wrath, anger, clamor, and evil speaking be put away from you, with all malice. And be kind to one another, tenderhearted, forgiving one another, just as God in Christ forgave you. (Eph. 4:31-32)

And what happens when our spouse sins again? We forgive them afresh.

"The Parable of the Unforgiving Servant" begins with this key question and answer:

Then Peter came to Him and said, "Lord, how often shall my brother sin against me, and I forgive him? Up to seven times?" Jesus said to him, "I do not say to you, up to seven times, but up to seventy times seven." (Matt. 18:21-22)

Forgiveness is not a one-time act. It must be freely given to fulfill our marriage vows. Our pledge to "love and to cherish" our spouse, "for better for worse, for richer for poorer," requires a love like Christ's that forgives again and again.

Humbly Obey God's Commands

The fourth way to cure contempt is to humbly obey God's commands, just as Jesus humbly obeyed the commands of His Father. Sinful emotions must be brought under the bright light of the truth. We must judge our emotions by the truth.

After Paul issued the command to do nothing "through selfish ambition or conceit" and put on the mind of Christ (Phil. 2:3-5), he explained how Jesus "humbled Himself and became obedient to the point of death, even the death of the cross" (Phil. 2:8).

The mind of Christ was a mind of humble obedience. And this humble obedience showed itself by Him dying for a weak, undeserving bride who someone less humble than Him would be tempted to scorn.

Husbands are commanded to love their wives in this same way, which gives no place for contempt (Eph. 5:25-28). Similarly, wives are commanded to reverently submit to their husbands from the heart (Eph. 5:22-24, 33) which precludes contempt on their part.

Humble obedience to God, by its very nature, requires the setting aside of self rather than thinking more highly of ourselves that we ought. This is the key cure for contempt.

Repent and Be Refreshed and Reshaped

Humble obedience requires humble repentance. While Christ was sinless and has no need to repent, we are beset with sin and can only be cleansed of it and find peace through repentance. The Apostle Peter declared, "Repent therefore and be converted, that your sins may be blotted out, so that times of refreshing may come from the presence of the Lord" (Acts 3:19).

When unrepentant sin lies festering in our heart, we tend to lash out at others in indefensible arrogance. We attempt to take the focus off our dark hearts by treating others with contempt. But repentance blots out our black sins and, in John Gill's words, leads to "spiritual refreshment, joy, and peace."[7]

The command to repent of our sins is for our good. Obeying this command will re-shape us and bring blessing to our marriage. It will cleanse us of our petty pride and cause us to act with greater kindness toward our imperfect spouse.

We need to be reshaped in this way. And it's not a one-time event. The whole Christian life is to be marked by ongoing repentance which reshapes us more and more into God's perfect image. This change comes from repentance from dead works. This is how we are to make our way back to Eden and bring joy to our marriage.

---

7   Commentary on Acts 3:19: John Gill, *An Exposition of the New Testament, Vol. II* (London: Mathews and Leigh, 1809), p. 168.

Conclusion

As you are learning to paint, don't paint pictures of volcanic contempt for one another. Paint scenes of the humble and forgiving.

When your heart and emotions are driving you to contempt, confess them. Renounce those feelings. Repent of these ungodly emotions. They are in opposition to the laws of love. Put them to death. Go with the commands of God and humbly repent.

The commands themselves are "spirit and . . . life" (John 6:63). They energize the work of God in the heart of the believer. They teach us how to love and respond to the weaknesses of our spouse with true compassion. They dissolve contempt.

As we wake up each day, let us keep the sinful volcano of our heart quelled by following Christ's example: "His compassions fail not. They are new every morning" (Lam. 3:22-23).

Questions

1. Are there subterranean earthquakes of growing contempt that need to be acknowledged and repented of?

2. Have you recognized the truth that ungodly emotions require repentance, not cultivation?

A Closing Word

I hope these pictures, drawn from Scripture, will help you paint beautiful scenes of home life—scenes that represent the beauties of the kingdom of heaven; scenes that glorify God.

I've written these words with the hope that God will give you the grace to create a little piece of heaven in your marriage and in your home, "'not by might, nor by power, but by My Spirit' says the Lord of Hosts" (Zech. 4:6).